Breaking Ranks®

A Field Guide for Leading Change

FOR MIDDLE AND HIGH SCHOOL LEADERS

NATIONAL ASSOCIATION
of SECONDARY SCHOOL
PRINCIPALS
Reston, VA

NATIONAL ASSOCIATION
OF SECONDARY SCHOOL
PRINCIPALS

1904 Association Drive
Reston, VA 20191-1537
www.principals.org

Larry D. Bradley, *President*
Steven Pophal, *President-Elect*
Gerald N. Tirozzi, *Executive Director*
Lenor G. Hersey, *Deputy Executive Director*
Dick Flanary, *Senior Director of Leadership and Program Services*
Jeanne Leonard, *Senior Director of Marketing, Membership, and Sales*
Robert N. Farrace, *Director of Publications*
John R. Nori, *Director of Program Development*
Pete Reed, *Director of Professional Development*
Patti Kinney, *Associate Director for Middle Level Services*
Mel Riddile, *Associate Director for High School Services*
James Rourke, *Principal Author*
Tanya S. Burke, *Associate Director for Graphics Services*
David Fernandes, *Production Manager*

Design and layout by Lisa Schnabel

ISBN 978-0-88210-380-8

Contents

Preface

In 2004, NASSP released *Breaking Ranks II: Strategies for Leading High School Reform* followed closely by *Breaking Ranks in the Middle: Strategies for Leading Middle Level Reform (2006)* advising principals to look strategically at the areas of schooling over which they hold sway—and to make some important and necessary changes. Although the framework and recommendations offered by those publications remain critical and relevant, too often when implementing the reforms schools neglect to focus on the importance of altering school culture. This guide discusses how a school-based leadership team can lead the effort to change school culture, thereby allowing reforms to take hold, flourish, and be sustained. Leaders at all levels must improve the leadership capacity within the school and become more knowledgeable of and proficient with the tools and approaches employed by organization development experts.

Principals, teachers and other school leaders are dedicated professionals who believe passionately in educating *each* student. Despite a long history of reforms, however, not every school has "arrived" at the point of serving each student. Every school leader has studied and reviewed plans or implemented reforms that appear on the surface to be thoughtful plans promising substantive impact. Yet when plan becomes reality, the results are either less significant than expected, the plan itself is too difficult to implement, or the resources needed are missing. In effect, we become so obsessed with the plan that we lose sight of the outcomes, or perhaps most important, the resulting changes cannot be sustained.

Changing culture requires more than being the first person with a great idea. Transformations do not take place until the culture of the school permits it—and no long-term significant change can take place without creating a culture to sustain that change. Leaders at all levels must foster this transformed environment. The question for education leaders at all levels is this: How can we foster these cultural changes within schools so that we can lead improvement and enhance student learning?

A great idea does not a great culture make; however, great leadership teams can have a lasting impact. What will your school's leadership team do to create a culture of achievement that survives beyond your tenure? Seize the opportunity to demonstrate to others what most of us in education already know—that great school leaders have the will, expertise, and determination to create a culture that challenges and educates each student. Properly implemented, the *Breaking Ranks* framework can reach every student. Properly sustained, whole school improvement leads to high quality education for all.

Sincerely,
Gerald N. Tirozzi
Executive Director, NASSP

Acknowledgements

NASSP would like to thank the following people for their contributions to this guide:

- NASSP staff members Rosa Aronson, Karen Danto, Bob Farrace, Jan Umphrey, Dick Flanary, Josephine Franklin, Carolyn Glascock, Liz Goldsby, Jeanne Leonard, Pete Reed, and Judy Richardson for their guidance and review of this project. Special thanks go to Patti Kinney, John R. Nori, and Mel Riddile for their significant writing contributions to this guide.

- The Center for Secondary School Redesign team for its contributions to this book in both concept and content. Special thanks and acknowledgement go to Bill Bryan, vice president, and Joe DiMartino, president.

- James R. Rourke, consultant and principal author, for his ability to synthesize the thoughts of so many disparate voices.

- NASSP Middle Level Task Force Members: Maria Bradley, Ralph Burnley, Nancy Chodoroff, Rose Colby, Patsy Dean, Marguerite Early, Joan Fargnoli, Maureen Furr, Julianne Fondell, Steve Hoelscher, Ned Kirsch, Diane Lauer, Ken McEwin, Jane Muna, Amy Torres, Terry Wolfson, Springy Yamasaki

- NASSP members and Breaking Ranks trainers: Tom Evans, Ryan Champeau, John Miller, Michael Curran, Georgia Taton, Misti Taton, John O'Neill, Bobby Ashley, and Janice Koslowski

- Two school principals—one middle level and one high school—have been interviewed for this book. They are leaders of two schools that were selected as Breakthrough Schools on the basis of their efforts to improve student performance in especially difficult circumstances. We thank them for the time they gave to this process and for the work they have done in providing the best possible education to students at their respective schools.

  - **James Cashman Middle School** was selected as a Breakthrough School in 2008 because of its strengths in many areas, including but not limited to collaborative leadership, data driven decision making, school improvement planning team, professional development, teaming, and connections with families.

    Cashman is an urban school of 950 students in grades 6 through 8. Approximately 76% are Hispanic, 9% are Black, 7% are Asian, and 8% are White; 100% are eligible for the free and reduced-price lunch program.

■ **Stuart High School** was selected as one of the original Breakthrough Schools in 2004 because of increased attendance and graduation rates, improved literacy and mathematics performance as measured by state tests, a high functioning leadership team and highly successful programs for English Language Learners. (note: The accomplishments noted for Stuart High School have been sustained under a new principal since 2006.)

In 2004, Stuart was an inner ring suburban school of approximately 1,500 students 24% Asian, 13% Black, 31% Hispanic, 31% White; 54% were eligible for the free and reduced-price lunch program.

How to Use This Guide

This book will focus on the "how" of making *Breaking Ranks* changes become part of your school culture. You already know the "what" of school change—*Breaking Ranks II: Strategies for Leading High School Reform* and *Breaking Ranks in the Middle: Strategies for Leading Middle Level Reform* told you that—but this book takes the next step. **It is designed to provide middle and high school leadership teams with the knowledge, tools, and resources to help move their schools beyond changes in structure and operations and delve deeply into the mission, values, beliefs, and goals that compose the culture of the school.** Without an emphasis on changing school culture, the ability of any single reform to be sustained and to improve learning for all students will be severely compromised and most likely doomed. The school's leadership team can use this guide to promote collaboration and professional conversations among staff members—and between high school and middle level staffs—that move beyond the basics of curriculum articulation and emphasize the additional importance of personalizing the learning and the school experience for *each* student at *all* grade levels.

In Chapter 1, we will discuss change leadership and describe how effective leadership teams can create conditions that facilitate change. The activities described will be useful in implementing any of the *Breaking Ranks* recommendations you adopt to improve student outcomes. To help you lead that change, we have developed a diagram of the change process—the **Process Circle**—defined in Chapter 2. We will use the segments of the Process Circle to describe the elements of creating a culture for sustainable change. The diagram incorporates critical components that should come as no surprise to any school leader who is familiar with change. Although your team may have its own model to guide its efforts, those efforts must include all six of the steps. The circle is intended to graphically represent continuous activity and the possibility of multiple entry points and will help organize the segments of the change process.

Following the general discussion of the Process Circle you will find real-school stories in Chapter 3. To provide you with examples of change leadership concepts in action, two top performing principals were interviewed in detail. Both were highly successful in instituting major changes under challenging conditions. Their success is validated by positive student outcomes that have been sustained over time.

The remainder of this guide will provide greater detail for each of the steps of the Process Circle:

- Gather and Analyze Data to Determine Priorities (Chapter 4)
- Explore Possible Solutions (Chapter 5)
- Assess Readiness and Build Capacity (Chapter 6)

- Create and Communicate Improvement Plan (Chapter 7)
- Implement the Plan; Monitor and Adjust (these steps combined in Chapter 8).

Caveat: Although the format requires us to describe the change steps in a sequential fashion by chapter, in reality change is rarely so neat, well defined, or linear. Situational demands and the culture of the school will require that adjustments be made. However, the sequence presented will make it easier to plan for and engage in activities that support and build on each other over time.

Each of the chapters describing a step of the process circle employs a common content format (and a consistent graphic):

- **Overview** of the step (e.g., Gather and Analyze Data to Determine Priorities), what it means, why it is important

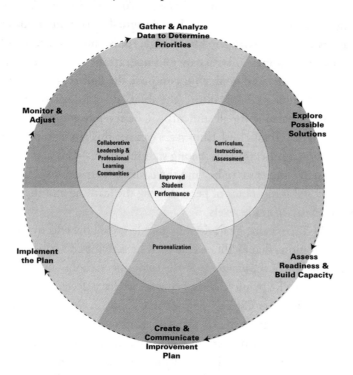

- **Change Leadership Activities** associated with the step, especially in the areas of data collection, collaborative leadership, infrastructure capacity, communication and buy-in, and professional development. The **Activities Matrix** in each chapter should be discussed and completed by your team. A blank chart for you to complete can be found next to the sample matrix. Spending the time to contemplate, discuss, and properly complete this chart within each of the chapters will help to ensure that your team has considered most areas related to the initiative. A sample of what a combined activities matrix might look like can be found in the last section "Tying It All Together."

■ **Challenges and Tips** will help you anticipate some typical pitfalls and propose some strategies for avoiding them.

 ■ **Change Leadership Tools** will be offered to help you with each step, for example, to help you gather and analyze the data needed to establish goals. Not every tool will be appropriate for your school so be discerning. Additional tools that can be conveniently completed online are also available at www.principals.org.

 ■ **When Things Go Wrong** stories will be interspersed throughout this guide to share reforms that didn't achieve the desired results. Those stories will be critiqued to help you avoid similar pitfalls and to highlight areas to consider during planning and implementation.

A final word before beginning to read…

This guide is focused on process, but that does not mean that your team should allow yourselves to be bogged down in the process. The tools in this book are designed to help your team achieve the desired outcome, not for the sake of engaging in the process. Complete all the steps in the process circle, but remember that not all tools and all suggestions offered will be relevant to your team's circumstances.

1 Focus on "How"

If you attempt to implement reforms but fail to engage the culture of a school, nothing will change.

—Seymour Sarason

As a school leader, you are all too familiar with the problems associated with the reforms du jour. Some reforms are conceptually sound but poorly implemented, others should never have been seriously considered. Examples abound—a flexible, block schedule is in place but instruction is delivered in 45-minute segments, interdisciplinary teams have common planning time but teachers fail to interact to address the instructional needs of the students, advisory time is used as a study hall, or participation in advanced classes does not reflect the school's demographics. With the tremendous amount of time, effort, and resources that are being devoted to educational reform, school leaders must develop their capacity to guide schools in making deep, meaningful changes that result in higher student achievement that can be sustained over time.

The question is not whether every school should improve—every school can and should. Rather it is a question of degree or area of emphasis. Whether you work in a school "in need of improvement" or a school where things are going *relatively* well or even very well, closing the achievement gap and addressing the needs of each student should be the centerpiece of your planning. Where does a leadership team start? Your leadership team and staff members have examined the data and planned a course of action that is based on what they think is best for students. But things feel disconnected—as if you are stringing together a series of actions and programs but getting nowhere. And while many of the things you are trying may be good in and of themselves, without a master plan connected to a vision, it's like trying to put together a giant jigsaw puzzle without the picture on the box to guide you.

Breaking Ranks II (2004) and *Breaking Ranks in the Middle* (2006) provided a framework to help schools become more student-centered by personalizing programs, support services, and academic challenges for every student. These publications identified three core areas for improvement:

- Collaborative leadership and professional learning communities
- Personalization of the school environment
- Curriculum, instruction, and assessment.

Each core area includes a number of recommendations specifically designed to make schools more challenging for and responsive to each student. Figure 1.1 demonstrates graphically how each core area relies on success in the others.

Figure 1.1
Connecting Breaking Ranks Recommendations in School Renewal

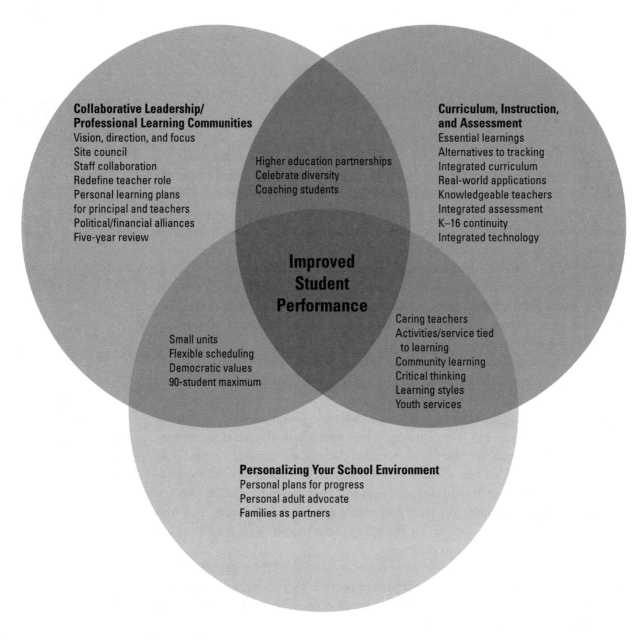

**Collaborative Leadership/
Professional Learning Communities**
Vision, direction, and focus
Site council
Staff collaboration
Redefine teacher role
Personal learning plans
for principal and teachers
Political/financial alliances
Five-year review

Higher education partnerships
Celebrate diversity
Coaching students

**Curriculum, Instruction,
and Assessment**
Essential learnings
Alternatives to tracking
Integrated curriculum
Real-world applications
Knowledgeable teachers
Integrated assessment
K–16 continuity
Integrated technology

**Improved
Student
Performance**

Small units
Flexible scheduling
Democratic values
90-student maximum

Caring teachers
Activities/service tied
to learning
Community learning
Critical thinking
Learning styles
Youth services

Personalizing Your School Environment
Personal plans for progress
Personal adult advocate
Families as partners

These recommendations emphasize the importance of engaging students in order to improve performance and success—and keep them from falling through the cracks. Although initiatives at the high school *can* clearly counter poor performance and habits from earlier years, the path to disengagement begins early in a student's academic career. A study of one urban district indicated that sixth graders who attend school less than 80% of the time, receive a poor final grade from their teachers in behavior, and are failing either mathematics or English are at high risk for dropping out in high school. The predictions are startling. Statistically, eighth graders who:

- Fail English have only a 12% likelihood of graduating from high school
- Fail math have a 13% likelihood of graduating
- Have high rates of absenteeism have only a 13% chance of graduating, and those with poor behavior will have a 20% chance (Balfanz, Herzog, & MacIver, 2007).

Similarly, compelling data regarding the need to promptly and forcefully confront disengagement comes from ACT. ACT data show that

fewer than 2 in 10 eighth graders are on target to be ready for college-level work by the time they graduate from high school. This means that more than 8 of 10 eighth-grade students do not have the knowledge and skills they need to enter high school and succeed there.…[S]tudents who are not prepared for high school are less likely than other students to be prepared for college and career by the time they graduate from high school. So although the gates of high school are technically open to all students, for more than 80 percent of them the door to their futures may already be closed. (ACT, 2008, p. 5)

The good news is that middle level and high schools following the *Breaking Ranks* framework are achieving success as exemplified by the MetLife Foundation-NASSP Breakthrough Schools. These schools are the outliers—the schools that have launched initiatives to help overcome the challenges and deficits posed by disengagement. The Breakthrough Schools project identifies, showcases, and recognizes middle level and high schools that are high achieving or are dramatically improving student achievement and serve large numbers of students living in poverty. Selection criteria are based on a school's documented success in implementing strategies aligned with the three core areas of *Breaking Ranks*. These schools have increased student engagement by using the *Breaking Ranks* framework to address the "what" of school reform and have succeeded in making the sustainable changes necessary to improve student achievement.

As the interconnectedness of the Venn diagram on page 6 implies, however, the "how" of changing the culture to foster these and other reforms is crucial and too often is given short shrift. The remainder of this field guide will focus on the "how" of reform.

"What" to Change vs. "How"

Relationships are critical to everything we do in life, personally and professionally. We ignore their importance at our peril. Think for a moment about your personal interactions with friends or family. Even the most commonplace events—a dinner, a trip to the store with the kids, an afternoon hike—have the opportunity to foster dynamic

"[Secret One, Love Your Employees] is not just about caring for employees. It is also about what works to get results. It is about sound strategies linked to impressive outcomes. One of the ways you love your employees is by creating conditions for them to succeed."

—Michael Fullan,
The Six Secrets of Change

relationships and lasting memories that can maintain those relationships during challenging times. How we comport ourselves during these commonplace times is often significantly more important than what we are actually doing. Likewise, in our professional interactions, the "how" is just as important—even when undertaking activities that are routine.

It is how we address the commonplace, the seemingly minor initiatives or small changes that will allow more significant activities to occur. These minor initiatives no longer seem minor when they foster a culture capable of tackling larger initiatives. Once the leadership team has helped create this culture, external influences or a change of principal will have minimal impact.

Most educators, when presented with good data, will agree on what needs to be done to turn things around (e.g., effective teaming, flexible scheduling, advisories, and differentiated instruction). Why is it then that most major change initiatives do not meet expectations or fail outright, whether in education, business, nonprofits, or government organizations? In most cases, it's not that people weren't smart enough, or didn't agree on what should be done, or didn't have the best of intentions. The reason is more commonly that they didn't know how to implement change effectively and how to sustain it.

Figure 1.2
Implementation Success Relies on How

20% of Successful Implementation Relies on What

Differentiated instruction
Personal learning plans
Advisories
Common planning time
Flexible scheduling
Activities/service tied to learning
K–16 continuity
Small units
Real-world application

80% of Successful Implementation Relies on How

Data collection and accurate analysis
Collaborative and distributed leadership
Assessing readiness and ability to build capacity
Values alignment
Professional development
Project management
Communication and buy-in
Role clarity and design
Monitoring and adjusting

Success is dependent mostly on how things are done, and in particular, how effective communication is, how much buy-in is obtained, and the degree to which everyone understands how roles will change as the initiatives are implemented. An authoritative leader can get something in place by decree, but it won't be implemented correctly and likely won't be sustained. The items in the left column in Figure 1.2 are reflective of the what—an initiative that might be selected to improve student outcomes. Although you can't move forward until the what is set, the items in the right column—the how—are the primary determinants of your success, the key change process elements. When people reflect on initiatives that didn't meet expectations or were dropped after a short while, they will invariably identify one or more of the items in the right column as being the primary cause. The tragedy of this is that with every failed initiative, the "change history bank account" decreases in value, making the chance of success for the next change initiative even slimmer. So where does your school start? In the following chapter, a process model—the *Breaking Ranks* Process Circle—will help teams discover where to start and what steps should be incorporated into any reform initiative.

I run institutes for educators on a regular basis. The last one was on advisories—how to design and implement them. I had 25 participants in the workshop. At the start of the first day, I asked how many participants were familiar with advisories. All 25 raised their hands, which surprised me a little bit. I then asked how many had advisories in their schools. Once again, everyone raised their hands, which surprised me more than a little bit. I then asked them why they were at my workshop. To a person, they said their advisories weren't working, and in some cases they were failing so miserably they were even thinking of trying to find a different name for the program. By the end of the workshop, it was very clear that while every school had a good reason for selecting advisories as an appropriate intervention, to a school, how they were implemented was predictably a disaster.

—Jackie Proulx, former principal, coach, and technical adviser, CSSR

"Team" Is the Key to Lasting Change

Quiz time for our leader reader. Read the paragraph below and answer the questions.

Student achievement has historically been high in your school but your population has changed dramatically. You have many new students and a significant number of English language learners (ELL). The ELL students who have been with you for only a short time are having trouble meeting district standards. Tension is high due to both the unstated and overt pressures exerted from the central office and the state. There are a number of possible solutions but all require significant change and lots of unknowns. Regardless of the change, it promises to be a messy business and someone or a group of someones isn't going to like it. What should you do to make the change successful?

Circle all that apply.
A. Develop the best course and strategy yourself and then seek buy-in.
B. Collect data from multiple sources to provide clear direction as to which initiative(s) to embrace and to build support for the direction once taken.
C. Make sure the perceived success of the initiative is motivating.
D. Embrace resistance as a good thing but address it quickly.
E. Build in "quick wins."
F. Expect major change to take 1–2 yrs and another 1–2 yrs. for it to become sustainable.
G. Help everyone define and understand his or her role.
H. Be transparent by communicating often and effectively.
I. All of the above.
J. All of the above except for A.

Answer: J. Most educational leaders would answer this correctly on a multiple-choice test, but *in practice* many have proven to be less successful—often arriving at strategies and solutions solo before working with a team to determine approaches. There are many *seemingly* justifiable reasons that one might try to go solo: the belief that there is a moral imperative to make change any way possible, a principal new to the school with a mandate to shake things up, failure to meet AYP, perceived inertia of staff, and so on. Unfortunately, reform history demonstrates that improvements derived from changes forced from the top will likely be short-lived. Principals can work with others to create a climate and culture that will foster significant and sustainable change—but principals cannot actually achieve that result by themselves. As a principal and leadership team your goal should not be to get everyone to toe to your line, but to arrive at a line together. The more leaders you help to create—both staff members and students—the more sustainable will be the thrust for excellence in your school. This type of collaborative leadership will also create the climate and conditions for optimum performance.

Culture Shift Supplants "Quick Fix" Mentality

"Leadership is the capacity to translate vision into reality," notes Warren Bennis (2008). To accomplish this translation, perhaps the most critical skill the school principal can bring to the table is that of understanding and managing the complex changes that must occur if schools are to improve. What is required is "deep change (that) alters the system in fundamental ways, offering a dramatic shift in direction and requiring new ways of thinking and acting"—what Marzano Waters, and McNulty (2005) refer to as "second-order" change. What most schools instead produce is "first-order" change: "incremental change (that) fine-tunes the system through a series of small steps that do not depart radically from the past" (p. 66).

The sad fact is that many of the changes being implemented are short lived with no lasting results. By focusing on the process as well as the reform initiatives, we hope to upend the oft-expressed sentiment coined by Irene Peter, "Just because everything is different doesn't mean anything has changed."

For too long educators have looked for a silver bullet that will solve schools' problems. A good idea is read or heard at a conference, brought back to the school, and implemented immediately. In the urgency to solve the problem, changes have been implemented without thought to the big picture. As a consequence, things may look different, but nothing of significance has really changed. School leaders who wish to move beyond this quick-fix mentality must do two things. First, they must recognize the critical role that a school's belief system plays in the sustainability of school improvement efforts, and second, they must carefully examine the process they are employing to implement the change.

Fullan (2004) described this type of change as the reculturing of schools. "Sustainability is very much a matter of changes in culture: powerful strategies that enable people to question and alter certain values and beliefs as they create new forms of learning within and between schools, and across levels of the system" (p. 60). Changing the attitudes, values, and beliefs that drive a school requires courage and effort. Underpinning this shift must be the core belief that each student should be challenged to achieve at high levels.

Culture is like the auto-pilot or mindset of a school. It is a combination of all the attitudes, beliefs, and values that guide the behavior of those in the school. Unless the programming for the auto-pilot is changed, the school will repeatedly return to its prior ways of operating and no real change will take place. For example, some researchers believe that punitive grading systems are a major contributor to decreased student motivation. Teachers who believe that grades are a lever to force students into improving will behave one way. Teachers who believe that grades are tools to use to encourage students to learn and improve will behave in a quite different manner. Unless the staff changes its mindset about grading and the purpose of grading, little real change will take place.

If changes in school culture are to occur, it is crucial that all efforts be collaborative in nature, but that does not diminish the role of the school principal as the leader of the process. In addition, while communication and buy-in are essential, there are times when consensus cannot be reached by a larger team, which may require that the leadership team make a decision. Because culture is driven by the physical conditions, rules, policies, practices, and the like that affect the culture, an open discussion of what will change and how it will change is necessary. Making decisions transparent is essential to the success of any endeavor.

A report by the Wallace Foundation (Leithwood, Louis, Anderson, & Wahlstrom, 2004), found that school leadership is "second only to teaching among school-related factors in its impact on student learning" (p. 3) and that the indicators of effective leadership are the result of three practices: setting direction, developing people, and redesigning the organization.

To understand why a defined process for changing the culture is so important—in some instances as important or more so than the actual change—it may be instructive to look at the experiences of a school that was unable to sustain success because of what some would consider a flawed process. It should serve as an eye-opener, a warning to those who want to embark on initiatives without first creating a culture to support it. In Chapter 2, the reader will find a recommended model—the *Breaking Ranks* Process Circle—to help schools avoid these pitfalls and put the school on a path to successful implementation of initiatives.

In the scenario that follows, the proposed changes made sense on the surface and at least some support had been established for the changes. Let's look at where it seemed to be going well but then became unsustainable. As you read this account, keep in mind

Fullan's *Six Secrets of Change*

1. Love Your Employees
2. Connect Peers with Purpose
3. Capacity Building Prevails
4. Learning Is the Work
5. Transparency Rules
6. Systems Learn

—Michael Fullan, *Six Secrets of Change*

Fullan's (2001) assumptions about change:

1. **Do not assume** that your version of what the change should be is the one that should or could be implemented.
2. **Assume** that any significant innovation, if it is to result in change, requires individual implementers to clarify their own meaning.
3. **Assume** that conflict and disagreement are not only inevitable but fundamental to successful change. Smooth implementation is often a sign that not much is really changing.
4. **Assume** that people need pressure to change. It is helpful to express what you value in the form of standards of practice and expectations of accountability, but only if coupled with capacity-building and problem-solving opportunities.
5. **Assume** that effective change takes time. It is a process of "development in use."
6. **Do not** assume that the reason for lack of implementation is outright rejection of the values embodied in the change or hard-core resistance to all change.
7. **Do not** expect all or even most people or groups to change. Progress occurs when we take steps that increase the number of people affected.
8. **Assume** that you will need a plan. Evolutionary planning and problem-coping models based on knowledge of the change process are essential.
9. **Assume** that no amount of knowledge will ever make it totally clear what action should be taken.
10. **Assume** that changing the culture of institutions is the real agenda, not implementing single innovations (pp. 122–124).

Full Retreat

The urban high school had been one of the top schools in the area. But after race riots in the 1960s and continued demographic changes, student performance went steadily downhill. By the 1980s, no performance standards were being met. To improve performance, the decision was made to establish *one* small learning community of 300 students within the school (total population of 1,500). Permission was obtained from the union to reduce teaching load and increase planning time for this subgroup. Performance of these students improved for a number of reasons (e.g., increased planning time, better teachers being assigned to the group and receiving additional technical assistance, and the more savvy parents working to have their children enrolled in this group.)

A new principal came on the scene in the mid 1990s. She saw two things:

- The students in the small group performed better

- The teachers who were not part of the small group had become resentful of the reduced teaching load and extra technical assistance provided to teachers who were.

The principal decided that since the small group was working well, the whole school—students and teachers—would benefit from being divided into four smaller learning communities. In addition, she

- Decided to implement advisories (and received a year-long planning grant from the district to make it happen)

- Received approval from the union for the smaller learning community design and advisories

- Sent out an RFP to the teachers to devise four academically themed communities and asked them to indicate their smaller learning community of choice.

So far, so good—the union was on board, and the teachers were happy they were being asked to be part of the planning process. The principal received four proposals from four groups of teachers and decided to move forward on the four proposed communities (liberal arts 1, liberal arts 2, sciences, and leadership). There were a few teachers who did not engage in the process, and they were assigned by the principal to one of the four groups. The original small group remained intact as one of the liberal arts communities.

On the surface, the plan looked great, and the principal received a lot of praise and recognition for the design. However, problems started immediately upon implementation. The extra planning time and reduced teaching load were not approved because of a lack of resources. As a result, not only did the new groups not get common planning time, but the original small group lost their planning time and reduced teaching load. In addition, although technical assistance was available to some degree, it was diluted across the four communities.

Teachers became disenchanted quickly because they felt the advisories and the smaller learning community design, which included a requirement for common planning time (but not reduced teaching load), required extra work for which they were not being compensated. It was not what they signed up for! The union, despite having agreed to the design, sided with the teachers. The situation became increasingly hostile; the principal felt overwhelmed and wasn't able to facilitate a solution to reduce the problems. She became increasingly stressed and took on a bunker mentality—spending all her time in full retreat behind her office door. Given the problems, she was relieved of her job by the central office and left the district. Shortly after that, the continued failure of students to perform to standards resulted in the state taking over the school and appointing a special master to run the school.

A Critique

It is very difficult to capture stories like this without a certain level of bias—and certainly in a case like this it would be difficult to capture all sides of the story. As such, we will stick to general critiques of this as a fictional story on the basis of the text presented rather than a factual case history.

Why did such an auspicious start end in disaster? The principal was reported to have said, "I can't understand how anyone could object to what is obviously such a great design!"

Although, to borrow Ted Sizer's (2002) words, you "have to change fast enough to keep gravity from pulling you back," planning must be spread out over a reasonable period of time to ensure that the impact of change is not underestimated. In this case, both the principal and the union failed to adequately analyze the potential sources and amount of resistance. Not only that but a year wasn't enough to get it right. The chances for success may have been improved by a well-defined process that to a far greater extent accounted for a change in school culture. That process might have included these items:

- Developing a plan for quick wins that would support the value of the changes for both teachers and students.

- Ensuring the case for change was strong enough for all stakeholders. In this case, the cost of change was immediately perceived by teachers as too high compared to the payoff. While the payoff may have been perceived as real for students, the payoff for teachers was not clear or high enough.

- Developing a formal communications plan to promote acceptance/approval/buy-in. In this case the principal didn't stay the course. While difficult to say in hindsight, perhaps if the communications had been better and resistance anticipated—especially when things got tough—the situation might have improved even in the face of opposition.

- Creating a stakeholder team to be the engine of change. This team could have conducted a role-design analysis for people affected by the change. Had stakeholders been involved in this process, there would have been more buy-in and increased role demands would have become obvious early on—and could have been dealt with appropriately.

- Understanding how policies, procedures, and practices would be impacted by the change. Because this impact wasn't planned for, adjustments weren't made.

- Understanding the issues associated with district-school alignment and how the associated barriers can sometimes be difficult to surmount.

> *"A vision of what might be plus a dissatisfaction with what is must be greater than the cost of change."*
>
> —Garmston and Costa

Reviewing challenging situations in hindsight is much easier than facing them as this principal had to do once the plan was already in place. This lesson and the real school stories throughout this guide are designed to help ensure that leadership teams prepare for significant changes before they begin to initiate them. In addition, this story demonstrates the importance of preparing individuals on leadership teams with the appropriate individual and team skills. The principal had little understanding of, and no model for, the change process; therefore, technical assistance around the change leadership process was not sought even though it may have improved the situation. The principal retreated in the face of pressure perhaps because she did not have the sophisticated influencing skills needed to reduce the conflict and get people on board. Could all of these have been addressed through professional development? Perhaps. Could this story have had a happier ending if a detailed process requiring a thorough vetting of the issues had been followed? It is certainly more likely. That is not to say that the principal might not have had a detailed plan—only that the detailed plan may not have addressed all of the important issues.

2 The Promise of Success: The Process Defined

Gladwell argued…that minor alterations, carefully conceived and adeptly enacted can produce major consequences for individuals, organizations, and communities.

—*Barry Glassner, as quoted in* The Tipping Point

Teams and their performance are crucial to your school's success. In days gone by, schools were judged on the performance of individuals. Their task was to sort students for success and their reputations rested upon a few "star" teachers who were masters at their crafts but operated as independent contractors. Today, schools are judged by the achievement of all students. Success depends on the collective performance of the entire staff and teams of teachers working together to ensure the success of all students. The best school leaders create environments in which teams are able to flourish.

Leaders who believe in their staff—that they are self-motivated, that better decisions are made collectively, and that buy-in and cooperation are more important than control—will promote a culture characterized by collaboration, trust, mutual respect, shared decision making, and a sense of ownership and shared responsibility. On the other hand, leaders who believe that people must be motivated, supervised, directed, and controlled will foster a hierarchical school culture characterized by top-down decision making, low trust, and a focus on control (McGregor, 1985). Although the latter type of leadership *may* supply short-term results, it may also lead to long-term resistance in other areas and a lack of interest in sustaining important long-term reforms. Be it driven by new leadership, external mandates, or a new direction inspired by existing leadership, change will only be effective if the proper conditions are created for *Breaking Ranks* reform.

While guiding your school from a "business-as-usual" mentality to one of continuous improvement, your team would be well advised to focus on shared vision and collaborative leadership. Schools are complex social systems and every school has its own DNA. Two schools with similar demographic profiles often function much differently from each other. Literacy, science, and math programs that worked well in one school may achieve only marginal success in others. Approaches must be adapted to the complexities of the individual school or the good ideas will never be put into practice.

> *As a complex institution, [a school] comprises many interlocking parts. Alter one element and you affect others. Thus, the recommendations...are best viewed as a series of connected proposals that in many instances depend on implementation in one area for success in another.... Piecemeal change may lead to some positive results, but it is not apt to be as effective as efforts that reach into the various parts of the system, in other words, systemic reform. [Schools] need more than tinkering.*
>
> —Breaking Ranks: Changing an American Institution

Changing the DNA of a school—trying to effect synchronous schoolwide change—is at best a risky proposition. Teachers have seen leaders and fads come and go, so they are appropriately skeptical. Leaders can't afford big mistakes, yet improved teaching and learning requires leaders to take risks and encourage innovation.

The good news is that we don't have to learn by trial-and-error. We can learn from other people's experiences, but only if we understand what will work for our school and when. As with diets, people are more likely to stick to a plan that matches their personalities, preferences, and lifestyle. In schools, no program or initiative will work unless the staff will "work the plan."

Moving Beyond 1,000 Demands

As a principal or member of the leadership team you likely have two things on your mind on any given day:

1. Simply making it through another day characterized by a thousand demands spiced with a few crises here and there
2. Helping each of your students produce significant achievements in his or her academic and personal lives.

The latter can seem beyond reach when you have so much on your plate—including an entrenched culture whose inertia rivals the greatest mountains. Even if people aren't happy with the current situation, they are much more likely to stick with the devil they know, the well-defined current state box below, rather than venture onto new ground with unknown borders. (See Figure 2.1.)

Figure 2.1

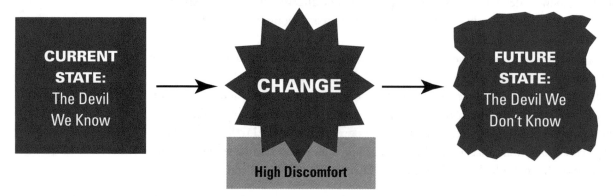

The **promise of long-term success** and higher student achievement will help your team begin to move that mountain and see beyond the high discomfort of change to a better future for students and the staff. The "Full Retreat" story in the previous chapter provided an example of a principal who had seen beyond the thousand demands and who developed an ambitious plan to improve the academic achievement and personal lives of the students. While the best of intentions did not prove to be enough; other profiles throughout this guide demonstrate there is hope that mountains can indeed be moved—with **great intentions, great leadership,** and a **great plan implemented properly**. As one school found, changes consistent with the *Breaking Ranks* recommendations can lead to dramatic change:

> The new principal walked into a high school where 91% of the students were eligible for free or reduced-price meals, 85% were minority, 20% were children of migrant farm workers. Only 8% were meeting standards in writing, 20% in reading, and 4% in math. Parent involvement was very low, with fewer than 10% present at parent-teacher conferences. Violence was the highest in the region. The graduation rate was 58%. However, within eight years, the numbers changed dramatically—66% meeting writing standards, 76% reading, and 31% math. Violence dropped to the lowest of the high schools in the region. The graduation rate jumped to 95%. A remarkable success story that was accomplished through student advisories and student-led conferences that included 100% parent attendance.

The realistic hope of success—a motivating factor for everyone—must be fostered by the leadership team.

A Process to Build Culture and Achieve Results

Which comes first: creating a culture that will support a process of change, or implementing a process that creates a culture to support change?

We will sidestep this chicken-and-egg debate entirely. Instead, while acknowledging that a highly influential and charismatic leader with a good plan *might* be able to *begin* to foster a culture of change, a process that fosters a culture of change while pursuing the goal of improved student performance will consistently produce more favorable conditions to realize goals. Simply because the process is designed to produce a better culture, the process need not be devoid of substance. A good process will have the ability to motivate the entire school team around initiatives aligned not for the improvement of culture alone, but ultimately for improved student performance.

It is at that point of **improved student performance** that the interconnectedness of the three core areas of *Breaking Ranks*—collaborative leadership/professional learning communities; personalization; and curriculum, instruction and assessment—bring meaning to the process for change outlined below, hereafter referred to as the Process Circle. By thoughtfully addressing each of the areas of the circle you will be able to ensure that your initiatives have a well-defined process that not only allows you to implement initiatives but also to do so in a way that improves school culture and becomes sustainable. A synopsis of the process circle can be found on pages 20–21. The remainder of this guide will focus on each of the steps of the circle.

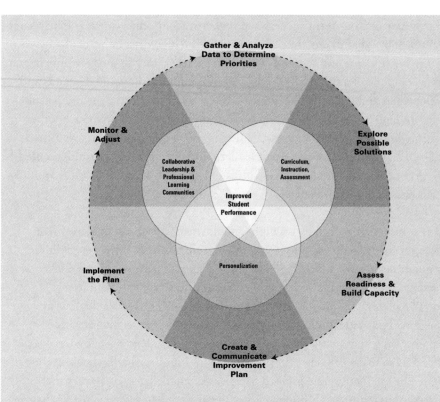

The Process to Break Ranks in Your School: A Synopsis

At the core, all efforts to change your school must ultimately be focused on improved student performance. To be successful, all steps of the *Breaking Ranks* change process must be based on a **shared vision**, promoted by **collaborative leadership** and supported by **professional development**.

1. **Gather and Analyze Data to Determine Priorities**

   Carefully examine all available data to **determine priorities**. To paint an accurate big-picture look at the school, data must be gathered from a wide variety of sources and used to determine the areas of greatest need. To be effective the data must be personalized—faces must be put on the numbers.

   Gather Data:
   a. *Demographic data:* Ethnic population, mobility rate, poverty indicators, parents' education, housing, etc.
   b. *Academic data:* State test scores; other testing data (SAT, ACT, PSAT, etc); district, school, and classroom assessments; failure rates; interim progress reports; observations of classroom practice—what's actually happening in the classroom; etc.
   c. *Diagnostic assessment data:* Reading, writing, mathematics (RTI)
   d. *Behavioral data:* Attendance, suspensions, referrals, expulsions, interventions, counselor visits, bullying issues, harassment, etc.
   e. *Miscellaneous data:* NASSP's satisfaction surveys (staff, parents, students—visit www.principals.org), surveys of business and community members, exit interviews and surveys, etc.
   f. *Student perception data:* Student shadowing, student forums, for example NASSP's Raising Student Voice and Participation model—RSVP.

Analyze Data:
Sort by subgroups; look for patterns, growth, and declines over time and correlations across subjects; equity of access to challenging classes; etc.

2. **Explore Possible Solutions**
   Based on the priorities derived from analyzing the data, **explore possible solutions** that will lead to improved student performance. Consider categories such as curriculum, instruction, assessment, professional development, equitable access to programs, academic support, and interventions as potential goal areas. Conduct site visits and talk with other school leaders. (See *Breaking Ranks II* and *Breaking Ranks in the Middle*.)

3. **Assess Readiness and Build Capacity**
   Determine what must be in place in order to successfully implement the needed changes. **Assess** staff needs, organizational structures, programs, and curricula to determine the school's **readiness** and overall **capacity** to address the identified priorities. **Build capacity** to address these needs through professional development, reallocating resources, and revising schedules.

4. **Create and Communicate Improvement Plan**
   Based on stakeholder input and the information gained from the previous step, establish goals for an **improvement plan** that is designed to improve student performance. Incorporate those goals into all aspects of school improvement planning and ensure clear **communication** with all involved parties.

5. **Implement the Plan**
   Just do it! (See *Breaking Ranks II* and *Breaking Ranks in the Middle* for proven strategies to guide implementation.)

6. **Monitor and Adjust**
   As the plan is implemented, determine regular check points to **monitor** progress. Repeat surveys as appropriate. As additional data is collected and analyzed, make **adjustments** or refinements as needed. Be sure to share results and progress.

Let's take a look at how one school's effective planning of a *Breaking Ranks* strategy and a culture of openness to new ideas fostered far-reaching changes that affected the entire school community and "map" the change to the *Breaking Ranks* Process Circle to give you a better idea of how initiatives can be implemented.

A Case Study of Sustainable and Effective Change

Although many organizational changes were implemented when Talent (OR) Junior High School converted to a middle school in 1990, one thing that remained the same was an arena-style format for parent-teacher conferences. Teachers gathered in a common space and parents were scheduled for 10-minute conferences with up to three teachers. Math and language arts teachers had long lines waiting to see them while others sat for long periods of time with no visitors. Attendance for the conferences was about 40%, conversations were hurried, the atmosphere was chaotic, and there was a severe lack of privacy—and although the conversations were about students, there was rarely a student in sight. If the school sincerely wanted to improve the communication process with parents to improve learning on a larger scale, something had to change.

Two teachers approached the administration with an idea. At a conference, they had heard about student-led conferences being held at the elementary level and they were interested in seeing if the idea would work at the middle level. These teachers wanted students not only to be a part of the conferences with parents but also to lead the conversations with parents during the conferences. Their hope was to get the students to take ownership and pride in presenting their strengths, weaknesses, and aspirations and to begin a more thoughtful and productive dialogue than the traditional parent-teacher conference.

Given the go ahead, the teachers researched the possibilities, devised a process, taught their students the necessary skills, and implemented the conferences. It was a resounding success and garnered the interest of others on staff. The school did continue to examine other ways to improve the conferencing process, but within a few years enough teachers were embracing the student-led process that the leadership team felt it was time to make a schoolwide shift to this way of conferencing.

Careful planning and collaboration as a staff helped ensure that the first attempt to use this as a schoolwide practice was a successful one. Together, the staff examined the best way to organize the conferences to ensure a smooth implementation. Equity of assignments was a major concern and many discussions were held to find a way to ensure that everyone would have a fair share of the workload. Out of these discussions came a structure that included every certified staff member (administrators included) serving as a conference facilitator for an equal number of students. A schedule was devised to provide a "drop-in" time period between student-led conferences to address concerns about parents interested in visiting specific teachers. A timeline for implementation was created so that expectations were clear. Even as staff worked together through it, some members were reluctant to try the new process. Their concerns were acknowledged and an evaluation of the process was promised. But the message was clear: the school was moving in this direction and everyone was expected to contribute to its success. Immediately after the first schoolwide implementation, staff, parents, and students were asked to evaluate the process and the results were used to adjust the process for the following year. And some of the initially reluctant teachers later became the strongest supporters of the process. Today, two principals later, the concept is a long-established practice at Talent Middle School and serves as a model program for others who wish to implement student-led conferences in their schools. The keys to sustaining this practice and making it an integral part of the school culture were the up-front planning and work that ensured a successful implementation the first time out and the continual evaluation and refinements that have occurred over the years.

Perhaps the most consistent message in the *Breaking Ranks* series is that schools must personalize the environment and the learning experience for each student. To do so, students must have opportunities to develop a sense of belonging to the school, a sense of ownership over the direction of their learning, and the ability to recognize options and make choices. This one initiative—the student-led conference—had far more dramatic consequences for the students and the school community because it did all of those things as well as adding the following benefits:

- Encouraged students to become more involved in their own learning

- Improved student engagement and parent attendance and engagement

- Created a structure that would not allow students to remain anonymous

- Allowed parents and teachers to develop a deeper appreciation for each student's abilities

- Encouraged student voice

- Improved parent-teacher-student communication.

Figure 2.2 maps the student-led conferencing initiative to the *Breaking Ranks* Process Circle. It offers an example of how your team might view this initiative from 30,000 feet. Each chapter of this guide, focuses on a segment of the process circle to help your team take a more detailed look at things to consider as your school launches initiatives.

Figure 2.2

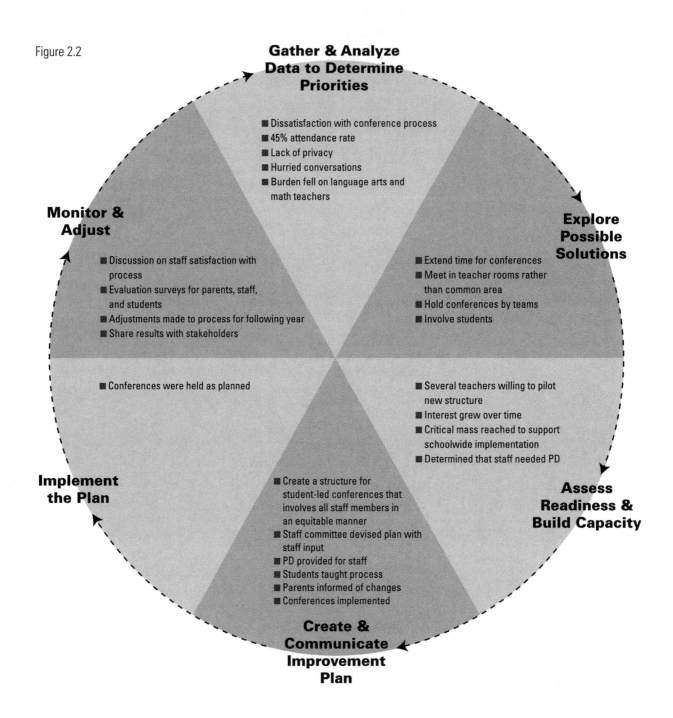

Gather & Analyze Data to Determine Priorities
- Dissatisfaction with conference process
- 45% attendance rate
- Lack of privacy
- Hurried conversations
- Burden fell on language arts and math teachers

Explore Possible Solutions
- Extend time for conferences
- Meet in teacher rooms rather than common area
- Hold conferences by teams
- Involve students

Assess Readiness & Build Capacity
- Several teachers willing to pilot new structure
- Interest grew over time
- Critical mass reached to support schoolwide implementation
- Determined that staff needed PD

Create & Communicate Improvement Plan
- Create a structure for student-led conferences that involves all staff members in an equitable manner
- Staff committee devised plan with staff input
- PD provided for staff
- Students taught process
- Parents informed of changes
- Conferences implemented

Implement the Plan
- Conferences were held as planned

Monitor & Adjust
- Discussion on staff satisfaction with process
- Evaluation surveys for parents, staff, and students
- Adjustments made to process for following year
- Share results with stakeholders

A well defined plan is essential, as is the ability to engage leaders at all levels within the school. Two stories of successful engagement and sustained improvement are found in the next chapter. The stories, captured in extended interviews with two principals—one high school, one middle level—highlight the importance of shared vision, collaboration and professional development. The excerpts depict, in the principals' words, the thought process and the activities in which each engaged at their respective schools. Both of the principals describe in detail what they did when faced with challenges, and how they accomplished enduring positive student outcomes.

As your team dissects the *Breaking Ranks* process, remember that breakthrough innovation is often hard for schools because it is difficult to turn ideas into practice. Principals and other members of the leadership team should be prepared to relinquish control and most important, to become comfortable with the idea that they do not need to have all the answers. The journey of finding answers as a school community is as valuable as the destination.

Chapter 2: The Promise of Success:
The Process Defined

3 In Their Own Words: Interviews With Two Principals

The data had changed the focus without my setting specific goals or saying what we had to do. The data got the focus off me and off [teachers] talking about their problems, and they started to talk about the students and what they needed.

—*High School Principal*

I n this chapter you will find the change story of one high school and one middle school. Each of the stories is told in such a way to align with a segment of the Process Circle. These stories are intended to be shared and discussed among your leadership team. To facilitate a text-based discussion, several questions and a protocol are provided.

Transforming a High School

I'm going to tell you about taking a high-poverty school that was labeled failing and making it a model school using a schoolwide literacy initiative. It took three years to put everything in place, and five years to make it permanent.

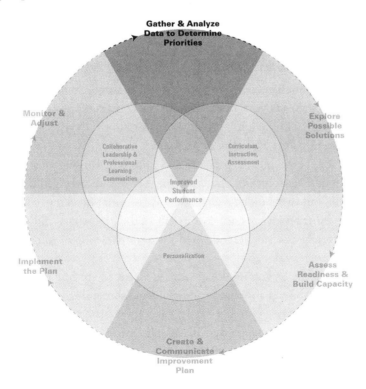

I knew that if we were going to be a high-performing school despite our high poverty, we had to be different from the way we had been, and we had to think differently about the students we served. I don't like stereotypes because of my experiences in school. I was a good student who went to college on an athletic scholarship because I was poor and couldn't go to college any other way. I wouldn't wear my letter jacket to class because I didn't want people to stereotype me. I carried that memory into this school determined to break the mold and be a good school—a great school.

The old mold was that poor students don't learn, that test scores can be predicted by zip code. The superintendent made it clear during our first meeting that the district wanted to change that. And when we were successful, he told me that our success was a result of no one telling the students and their teachers that poor students couldn't achieve at the highest levels.

The literacy initiative came out of my conversations with staff members soon after I became principal. I remember asking one of the teacher leaders what we needed to do to improve. She said that most of the students come from very difficult backgrounds and lived in poverty, had trouble learning, did not have a lot of family support, didn't come to school, and couldn't read. That conversation stuck in my mind for years.

I knew that she was pretty close about attendance; my high school had the lowest average daily attendance in the school system. That was data that was easy to find. I knew that students missed an average of 23.5 days per year—that's a month of school. When I asked her to explain what she meant about reading, she said that her students couldn't read the textbook and she had to adapt everything for them.

From other conversations, I learned that staff members believed that they were doing the best that they could, or so they had convinced themselves. Clearly, the staff was dedicated, hard-working, and committed to the students. However, unless we raised our expectations, many of our students would never graduate. For the sake of our students, we just had to do better.

The first step in the change process had to be to collect some data and find out what was going on. I knew the attendance was bad, but there wasn't any information on literacy. "They just can't read," Teachers would declare. And while I trusted what they were telling me, we needed data to show it.

The next step was meeting with my staff members. In my State of the School message at the beginning of each year, I talked about my conversations with staff members and what I had heard from them in individual conversations: the two things they had mentioned consistently were attendance and literacy.

I acknowledged the attendance problem and proposed forming an attendance committee to work on it. I set some goals at that time. I also acknowledged that there was a reading problem, but that I didn't really have any information except some state test scores that really didn't reveal the nature or extent of the problem. I told them the first step was to do a formal assessment, and when it was done, we were going to meet and go over the results.

But that was just the beginning. I had worked all my life to be a principal, and knew if I was going to be a change agent and really get something done, that standing up in front of a faculty once a year at a faculty meeting wasn't going to be enough. I needed to communicate more regularly with people. And I needed to focus on what was really important: teaching and learning. So I wrote a school newsletter every week. I did

Gather & Analyze Data

about 36 issues a year, probably 1,200–1,500 words an issue, about 50 to 60 thousand words a year. I used the newsletter as a vehicle to talk about a variety of topics, including literacy, and to recognize a teacher of the week and other items. Over the years, I went back to literacy quite a bit. It was a big commitment, but every Sunday afternoon, I wrote that newsletter. I was very proud of it. The teachers read it—they even named it. It accelerated the culture shift. They knew what I was thinking, they knew exactly where I was coming from and how my thinking was changing and evolving. That the most important thing was teaching and learning.

Create & Communicate Plan

I made the decision to go ahead with the assessment, and the people in the school were supportive. However, nothing is as easy as it first appears. Before we started the assessment, I got a call from the assistant superintendent who had heard that I wanted to test the students in reading. Her exact words were, "Why do you want to do that?"

She was afraid that I was looking for an excuse for low performance or that I was going to stigmatize the students. I had to assure her that I wasn't, that people kept telling me that the students couldn't read, but I had no evidence. I wanted to find out if students had a reading problem and, if so, the extent and nature of it.

When she told me we would have to meet with people at the central office, my first reaction was astonishment. It seemed like a normal thing to me, and she was acting like it was abnormal. I thought that there must be some hidden agendas or turf battles going on and I was stepping on toes.

At a meeting with about a dozen people from central office, I was grilled for about an hour about what I was going to do with the results. I told them that we were going to analyze the results to see what the scope of the problem was, figure out what we wanted to do, and develop a strategy. I explained that I didn't have a master plan at that point, because I didn't know the scope and the nature the problem.

That made the group more comfortable. They wanted to support me but also wanted to make sure I wasn't in uncharted territory and that the whole ship was not going to sink. They also needed to convince other people I was okay, that I wasn't going to assign students to some type of detention if they couldn't read. The elementary supervisor expressed some general concerns over the assessment, and I found out later that there was fear of finger pointing if students couldn't read and had matriculated through the schools. (Jumping ahead a bit, that turned out to be the case. When I presented the data, it started a firestorm of finger pointing and discussions in the school system.)

Assess Readiness

The good news was that the superintendent and her deputy agreed to let me go ahead with the assessment. I remember when the meeting was over thinking to myself, I know why principals don't innovate, it's intimidating.

The assessment went smoothly. We tested only general education students because we already had data on students who were in special education or were English language learners. The data showed that 76% of students were below the 39th percentile. One out of five were in the 1st to 4th percentile, almost four years below grade level. At that point I wondered why I took the job! The data was more than bad, it was frightening.

The teachers were curious and wanted to see the results, but I wanted to look at the impact of mobility before I presented the results to them. How many students had come from our feeder schools? I knew the first thing people were going to say was, "Well, they are not our kids. We never taught them." We found, however, that almost two-thirds of the students had been through our elementary and middle schools. Many had been at grade level in the third grade, but by ninth grade they had fallen significantly behind. I knew that was going to hit some people in the lower grades right between the eyes.

Finally, with the assessment and mobility data in hand, I presented the results. A lot of our students were below the 5th grade level in the 9th, 10th and 11th grades, and the textbooks were written at approximately the 11th grade level. The staff's response was similar to the initial reaction I had, which was one of surprise that it was as bad as it was. But some people felt validated.

I gave them copies so they could think about it more. In addition, I promised them the reading scores of every one of their students and asked them to put those scores in their grade books. That got a lot of buzz because it made the data real for them. With that data in their books, the problem was not the principal's opinion: it was fact, it was real, and it related to individual students. I fell back on my training. If you give high performing people data, just feedback, they are going to figure out a way to improve. I see teachers as people who were good students when they were in school, high performers, and when you give an achievement-motivated person data, they tend to want to improve; it's their nature.

I also wanted them to realize they could all be a part of the solution and volunteer to help improve the situation. At that point, I started to have department meetings. During an English department meeting, I remember a teacher saying, "I've got 18 students out of 24 in my English class that are 6th grade and below, how can I teach *Romeo and Juliet* to these students?" One of the teachers said, "Should we be teaching *Romeo and Juliet* to these students if they can't read? Should we even try?" After an hour one of the teachers said, "We've got to figure out a way to do it." My role was just refereeing… keeping the conversation going and letting the teachers do the talking, not me doing the telling.

The important thing was that the data had changed the focus, without my setting specific goals or saying what we had to do. Everybody understood we had to be at grade level. The data got the focus off me and off them talking about their problems, and they started to talk about the students and what they needed. When you talk about literacy in school, you are talking about the students and what the students can do and what skills they need; that changes the focus and eventually the culture.

Explore Possible Solutions

After speaking with many individuals, department chairs, and their teams, I proposed putting a literacy council together. I asked department chairs to recommend people in their departments, and included the chairs on the council as well. My goal was to change how we were doing things, to make them a part of the decision making. Since I had already set up an attendance committee, it made sense to have a literacy council. I wanted people who were interested, and I tried to get somebody from each department. We ended up with about 12 to 15 people on the council.

I remember the initial council meeting well. Everybody had looked at the data, and we continued to talk about the reactions people had to it. I wanted their opinions and responses to such questions as What do you think we need to do? We've taken the first step, what is the next step?

I had a definite strategy in mind, which was to start with data collection, present it so that it wasn't my opinion, let people start running in different directions, develop a partnership with an expert in literacy, and create a team—what I call a *skunkworks*. This was an experimental group of early innovators who want to do things differently, to try new things, and find out what works and what doesn't work. If it works it will spread, creating a kind of tipping point. (See p. 68 for more about skunkworks.)

I found that teachers love recognition, and by being a part of the skunkworks they felt special. They moved from observers to leaders to owners; they took ownership of the success of one another and of the outcomes.

To recap, my strategy was to:

- Ensure everyone saw the data
- Put the data for each student in every teacher's grade book
- Establish a literacy council that would be responsible for figuring out how to improve our students' reading from a big picture perspective
- Visit each department and challenge each teacher to build a strong literacy component into everything they did and supported them with professional development and support materials
- Hire a literacy coach who would bring in real expertise and support for teachers
- Create a skunkworks, a group of innovators to work with the literacy coach, who wouldn't be afraid to test out new ideas to find the ones best suited for us
- Support our literacy initiative through my newsletter.

At the time, I did not know a high school that had a reading program so there were no models. None of my colleagues knew of one. Adolescent literacy at that time had very few materials. If you tried to find an appropriate reader for adolescents, you would probably get something that was closer to kindergarten-level material. We were trying to invent the wheel as we were going along. We were being asked to do something with the kind of students that nobody else had really done before on a schoolwide basis. We had to create the tools we needed and be willing to do pilots and anything it took to move forward. I was in uncharted waters and willing to try a number of things to see what would work.

My initial impression of the school was that it was focused on the adults, and the students' needs were an inconvenience, something the adults had to work around, not work for. You know, the students didn't go to school, they didn't go to class, and they didn't know how to read. When they did attend, it was like an affront to the teachers. After the data were presented to the staff in that first meeting, the discussion was different from any earlier discussion because it was all focused on the students and their scores and their performance and how teachers could help them. They wanted to know what they needed to do to change what they were doing to meet the needs of the students. The data changed the focus without my setting specific goals or saying we had to do this; the staff came to the conclusion that everyone had to be at grade level.

When they put the students and the reading scores together, they went from intellectual understanding to emotional acceptance. They needed to see it everyday and be reminded of it, and the grade book was the best way to do it.

The literacy council, of which I was a member, was tasked with identifying what we needed to do. The goal the council set was to have all students at grade level by 11th grade for the state test—a thousand days from the time a student walked in the school to get them to grade level before they took the state test. In addition, some of the people on the council wanted to work together in the summer to put together some materials on reading strategies. Another thing they identified was to get professional development for the staff and materials to help the teachers.

With regard to professional development, my goal was to do job-embedded staff development once a month with our teachers. Every session was a teacher-led professional development activity, and not just a dissemination of information. And I wanted to get innovators working together. Let them take the data and start running in different directions, develop a partnership with an expert, and create a skunkworks.

I wanted to get activity going on multiple fronts, to challenge each department to identify what they were going to do to support improving our literacy and attendance. I emphasized literacy and attendance every chance I got. I coined the term "R-A-G-S to Riches." It's Reading plus Attendance means better Grades in a Safe School. All the teachers in the building could tell anybody outside the building what our school plan was. We kept it simple and very focused. If we could get the students to school and teach them good literacy skills, we were ultimately going to be more successful as a school.

Once we started, we had a number of things in motion. The reading council was looking at an overall school approach, while subject-area teachers were looking within their subjects. We had some experimental groups going on. They were just trying some things out, seeing what was going to work. We had little initiatives, for example, the English department decided to stop everything and conduct a reading session once a week, create a reading lab that all the 9th-grade English classes cycled through, established annual pre- and post- assessments. The school now does a reading test every spring. In addition, the literacy coach was making progress working with teachers.

The buzz was really generated by the literacy coach. She had gathered eight or nine people on the faculty that she could count on to try things out whenever she wanted to work with people. They were an ad hoc group—the experimental group. They would try things; some of them worked and some of them didn't. If they worked, we would talk it up at the faculty meetings and in the newsletter. Teachers did presentations in faculty meetings, which was some of the professional development we did that year.

When teachers on the literacy council came to me and said that they wanted to work together during the summer to put together some materials, I was able to secure some money for them. They came back with what I called the "Joy of Reading." They found every reading activity they could put in a book—which turned out to be not very useful, but it was the activity that counted because they came in and talked about it, and started taking leadership roles in the school and in the meetings. The literacy initiative was teacher-driven and principal-supported.

Although it was great the teachers were taking the lead, I did need to provide guidance on how to make their efforts pay off. With the Joy of Reading and its thousand strategies, I knew I had to get them to pare it down so I used an example of a program we had had in the school system on standards-based classroom instruction. The author had taken every classroom strategy imaginable, put it in a book, and given it to us. When I asked, "Now, how many of you are using this?" they just laughed. Everybody agreed. So they went to work and they picked the strategies and did a presentation at the faculty meeting. We introduced 10 strategies we expected everyone to know. During the school year we trained them how to use those strategies.

From the beginning, I was looking for successes to build on and to publicize. One of the teachers was having a lot of success with her students, getting them interested and motivated. Her students were making a lot of progress. She was a science teacher, and I wrote about her in the newsletter. She really went way out of her way to adapt instructional materials. A group of ESL students she worked with had exceeded the department average in her subject. She became one of our first heroes—a barrier buster, breaking preconceived notions of what students could or could not do.

The students said, "She won't give up on us, she won't let us fail." There were other early successes: a first year teacher who helped her students receive very high scores, a math teacher who helped her special education students do really well, a teacher who taught double block math with the lowest performing students and had a very high success rate.

This was all part of identifying the champions who did something that nobody expected could be done and changed attitudes as a result. In other words, if she could do it with those students, anybody could do it.

The key was to take those examples of success in some classrooms and do it as a whole school. Stereotypes were broken at faculty meetings where the art department presented literacy strategies that they used in art class and the music teachers and orchestra and band director did a presentation on integrating literacy strategies in music instruction. We were breaking down the old attitudes and belief systems one by one. We were reprogramming our auto-pilot. People walked out of there, and they just did not have any more excuses.

To reinforce this whole idea of breaking barriers and thinking differently, I did what we called a break-through and taught them how to do karate-style board breaking. The exercise took about two to three hours and the teachers learned to break boards to break through old barriers. I had the teachers write things on the board that they wanted to break through in their personal life, and in their professional life. Also, I had them break through some of the goals that we had about getting students to grade level and things like that. About 98% broke the boards but 100% tried, which was fascinating. That was a big risk on my part. I didn't know how these people were going to react to it. The message was that they were going to go there not wanting to do it. As a teacher I had to get them to want to do it—that's what they had to do with students everyday in their classrooms. It worked--it was a real motivator! The proof is that the people kept their boards as mementos.

Motivation is definitely important, but what really made a difference was coaching and development, such as monthly training for our teachers during their 30-minute planning period. We were concerned that teachers would not know how to implement the 10 strategies the literacy council had identified as most important and needed a way to follow up with the teachers to make sure that they understood how to apply them. The council set up a system of peer observations where people would voluntarily buddy-up with somebody else. It could be somebody in their department or somebody else, and they would agree to observe that person doing a particular strategy. If they needed assistance, they could ask the literacy coach. We laid out a guideline and said that, "We don't expect you to know any of this, it's our responsibility to teach it to you and to help you learn it."

It's typical for teachers to be concerned that somebody is going to check on them.

Assess Readiness/ Build Capacity

Monitor & Adjust

When there is an expectation laid on them, they either start arguing against it, they try to hide, or they push ahead. What I wanted to do was to eliminate the fear of failure—to convince them this is something everybody can do, and it was my job as a principal and the literacy coach's job to teach them how to use these strategies well. I made it clear that I didn't want anyone to be worried about failing. There was no failure. There was nobody getting rid of people because they didn't understand the strategies. Teachers had to do one thing, work with us. The job-embedded professional development turned out to be very effective for us, not only in literacy but also in the long-term in just about everything else we did. That was our model, and once a month during teachers' planning period, they could count on some type of professional development.

As I think back on all this, as the principal, I really had two roles:

- Setting the course for things we needed to do. Ultimately, I was the person accountable. I had to stick my neck out and be willing to get it chopped off.
- Removing barriers. External barriers, such as lack of resources and equipment, were getting in the way of things.

Assess Readiness/ Build Capacity

For every hour I spent setting direction, I probably spent five hours removing barriers. That also meant removing the mindset barriers—the attitudes and belief systems of people. Both roles were important because I could change people's attitudes but if they didn't have the equipment and the resources or if some policy was getting in their way, then they couldn't get anything done. Barriers became excuses. And with literacy, it is particularly important to eliminate excuses because literacy isn't a normal part of a high school environment. When you are trying to put something in place that is not normal, mole hills become mountains. My role was to remove barriers before they became mountains.

Monitor & Adjust

My philosophy about change and trying new things was also important. When you give people responsibility, you can't go in and take it away from them and start to intervene. We had to give our approach a chance. If it didn't fly, we all agreed that we would go back and look at it. Everything we agreed to try was open to discussion and change. There was nothing sacred. In fact, we literally did change or modify everything in some way each year.

When the data started coming in that first spring, the teachers were really excited—we were all excited about the results that we were getting. We started with the low-hanging fruit and got some quick wins. Teachers were starting to get excited about the fact that they could actually do it. They began believing that we can actually help students learn! And when we did our annual assessment and discovered that we were averaging two-year gains—every English teacher averaged a two-year gain with each student—we were very happy. We didn't sit on our laurels, though. We went back to find out from the teachers what was working and continued to improve.

Leading a Text-Based Discussion

Below you will find several questions that may help your team to participate in or lead a text-based discussion. (*Breaking Ranks in the Middle* offers complete guidelines for conducting a text-based discussion, page 281.)

The purpose of a text-based discussion is to enlarge understanding of the text, not the achievement of some particular understanding. Multiple perspectives create broader understanding and present possibilities for new insights and meaning. Be sure to provide each participant with a copy of the text (with page numbers on the copies) ahead of time so that all participants have time to thoroughly read the piece. Encourage them to highlight passages and jot down notes about what they're reading to share during group discussion or using the think-pair-share method. Very large groups should be organized into discussion groups of 8–12 participants to enable deeper discussion than is generally possible in large groups. Focus on questions such as: What are the implications of this text for…?

Text-Based Discussion Questions

1. When educators understand that poor students can achieve at the highest level, an important roadblock to success is removed. But the question remains, How can we fill in the gaps in learning that exist for so many students? What did this principal do to provide teachers with what they needed to improve kids reading levels? How did the staff members keep teaching *Romeo and Juliet* to the students?

2. This staff seemed to understand that change requires working through a process and takes time. How did this principal facilitate change? How can a staff's familiarity and understanding of the change process move the process forward and what are the potential roadblocks?

3. The principal in this scenario said, "…if you give high-performing people data…, they are going to figure out a way to improve. I see teachers as people who were good students when they were in school, high performers, and when you give an achievement-motivated person data, they tend to want to improve…it's their nature." Would the staff at your school respond similarly? Why? Why not? What was done by this principal to elicit this reaction from the staff? How was the idea that it's too late to turn things around for these students avoided?

4. Removing barriers so that work can get done and achievement can be accessed is essential to the process of facilitating change. What are some of the ways that the leadership team in your building can provide this support? What will happen if they don't?

Middle School Principal

Unlike many school districts, mine could place or change principals at any time during the year. You could find yourself in one school on a Friday afternoon and a new one the following Monday morning. That's what happened to me. I started my job as principal of an urban middle school in late January of the school year. When I announced my new position, my former colleagues said, "Oh, you are going to *that* school?"

The student population was roughly 1,200 students in sixth, seventh, and eighth grades and 85% of the students were of Hispanic descent. Most of the parents were shift workers with big families. I went from the middle school math/science magnet in the district to open a new magnet. The new school—my new school—had once been a good school, but by the time I arrived that was no longer the case. Test scores were not good.

The thing I noticed when I walked through the doors for the first time was how fabulous the students were. They were incredible. I remember hearing "please," "thank you," and doors opening for me, "Hi Miss!" They were so excited! I walked through the cafeteria and everybody was mixed at the tables. I had three self-contained special units—and even the severely multiple challenged students were in the cafeteria. It struck me as very much a community.

At first, I just tried to get my arms around everything, figure out what was going on. My first week, the whole school support team (SST) was visiting, so I just listened in. Listening to them I thought, "Wow, we have this great school!" I heard about our great reading programs, and the intervention programs, and mentoring, and how everyone was focused on "critical stance." Afterwards, I asked five staff members to explain *critical stance* to me. No takers. Apparently everyone was focused on it, but not exactly sure what it meant. So after I listened to all of this great stuff, I decided it was time to visit different classrooms.

In one classroom, the students were sitting at a computer, and the teacher was reading a newspaper. I went to another classroom where the students were all silent doing worksheets and the teacher was sitting at her desk. I made it a point to visit every classroom. What I saw floored me! Everything I had heard from the SST was all about how student centered the school was—but that wasn't what I found in the classrooms.

Those first two weeks on the job, I wanted to know what it felt like from our students' points of view. I literally followed several students for their entire day. In one case, I sat at a computer for half the day. I remember following one 8th grader and wanting to leave school by lunchtime. Boring, boring, boring! Boring bookwork, boring worksheets, no interaction in the classroom. I thought, "Wow, this is them everyday! I can't imagine doing that for 180 days." So that was part of the dynamic of where I focused first.

Fortunately, not every classroom was like that. Some were great and the students were really engaged. For example, one math teacher circled the room talking to the students, asking questions, checking in with small groups—all the things on a principal's checklist you'd want to see. It was just a nice feel in the room. It was a really low-performing class but there was authentic engagement in the classroom. How could we get that going throughout the school?

My philosophy has always been to do what's best for the child and not what's expedient for the adult. But I noticed that much of what was being done was adult centered.

Sure we had interventions—I had some sixth graders who were going to three different reading-intervention programs in one day! But I also had teachers who couldn't understand why there was no growth in reading.

A member of the state team asked me how I was feeling. I told him I was really surprised… what I was hearing from the adults wasn't happening in the classrooms. So we had a long talk, and he asked what direction I wanted to take with the school. We sat there for a couple of hours just talking.

I knew I needed more data. Teachers told me they had the data, but they didn't really. Some had nothing. Data would help me see what had to be done—and get everyone to buy in.

Gather & Analzye Data

I went to one of the regional people to get state AYP test data—three-year trends, everything for all three grades. I stayed those first few weeks until 9:00 or 10:00 p.m., because I couldn't get those things done during the day. I just sat at that computer and pulled random schedules of different students from different grades. Again, many students were in one, two, three reading intervention programs—plus they might still be in their regular reading class. On top of that, they were often pulled from an elective class to go into a reading intervention program. How could a child sit for half of their day in three reading programs? It was no wonder the students weren't getting any better. Now, I had a piece of paper that could give me any statistic I wanted about any student in the building, but it didn't tell me about the school, and I didn't want to make the same assumptions that everybody else did.

I found another problem: all the accelerated English classes were removed because the staff thought that our students were so low-performing. That put a knot in my stomach. The students may have been language challenged, but they were not stupid. Nobody was looking to raise the bar.

Chapter 3:
In Their Own Words:
Interviews with Two Principals

So how would we get things on the right track? It had to involve the in-house school improvement plan (SIP) team. I found that it had too few people on it—only the school librarian, the learning strategist, the remediation teacher, and the ELL specialist—and they wrote our school improvement plan. How could we improve if there weren't more classroom teachers involved? A special education person had to be on there, and grades 6, 7, and 8 all needed representation. I went through my whole staff list with my learning strategist and asked, "Who are my strong ones? Who are my weak ones? Who is going to be honest with me? Who is not?" I have the union secretary in my building, for example, and I needed her on board to influence the rest of the staff. Another teacher, new to the district, had a strong background in math and data. Those were the kinds of people I needed to expand the SIP team and make it work.

While building the SIP team, our next state test (CRT) was looming 12 weeks away. I knew we were going to fall to N4 (needs improvement, year four). At N5, the state would take over. With that on our doorstep, we needed to decide how we were going to approach and attack the test. I had to make decisions quickly about how to help my teachers understand what they needed to do. And I had to have their buy-in. If I didn't have qualitative and quantitative baseline data to share with them, then the decisions we made were not going to be relevant—they weren't going to be better than any of the decisions made in the past. Numbers aren't scary, but they can mean a lot of things, depending on how they are approached. I faced a huge task, but if we could be successful with the test, we could start turning other things around as well.

To make changes, particularly to improve the CRT scores in April, I had to involve more people than the SIP team. The staff had had it with changes and demands.

They also had plenty of staff development, but it was never taken to the next level. I needed them to apply the data—really think about it—and drill down and make decisions. Those students who sat in three reading intervention classes, for example, saw no progress. Somebody should have caught that. I asked my dean of students and my learning strategist about the attendance issue. They told me it was that the Hispanic girls didn't come to school, but the data showed they had a 94% attendance rate. It was the White males who had the attendance problem. There were lots of pieces, but nobody was putting the puzzle together.

With so little time before the CRT, I had to meet the whole staff—administrators and teachers together—so they had the full picture. An opportunity was available called Sprint for the CRTs, a set of extra resources to prepare for the CRT. Everybody was going to participate, not just the math teachers, not just the reading teachers. We were going to support the effort schoolwide.

The staff meeting was full. I was nervous. First, my philosophy: From here on, everything we do will filter through the question, Is this in the best interest of the students? I shared my background at both the middle level and the high school, my experience, and my belief that every child can learn—regardless of their background. I was honest with them without bashing anyone else, and I let them know that I needed their help and their expertise. We were in this together.

Transparency was an issue that had to be dealt with right away; apparently, many staff members felt that things were done behind closed doors. I used that first meeting to show them I did not do things that way. The daily class rotational schedule, for instance, was a big problem. But rather than my imposing a solution, the staff had to decide what to do with the schedule to improve test results. They—not I—voted and counted the votes. I had a few holdouts—I saw the eye rolling in the back and heard the side conversations—but that transparency led to buy-in. "I can't do this alone," I told them. "I don't know how. You know the students. You are in the classroom. I can give you the data, but you tell me what you need to turn it around."

I distributed data from the district and asked them what they saw in it. Many students came close to passing—the bubble kids. I agreed and asked them what we should do. I had already sorted the students by test scores, and we started talking about what approach to take. That is when they started talking to one another.

Too often, principals have great ideas and just want to *do*. But leading is really about listening. It took a lot of listening and balancing and saying, "Okay, A, B, C, and D work. We can keep those, but with the others, do we tweak them, fix them, or maybe get rid of some stuff that's not working?" At that very point, I wanted them to think about what they were doing and get them to start working together.

I had already seen the possibilities, but I needed it to come from them. That was when I told them about the Sprint for the CRTs and that we had only 63 days from that point until we took the tests. One goal I had when I walked into the meeting was to have a boot camp, which had worked for me before. I asked for volunteers for Saturday school to work with the bubble kids with no guarantee of pay, although there were some Title I funds and I promised to try. I asked them to give up two Saturdays; although they were skeptical that the kids would show up, teachers committed.

Leaders started to emerge—and not the leaders who were there before. Quiet people stood up and volunteered to help any way they could. I saw the ball rolling, and many of those new leaders were the people I tapped to be on our SIP team, which I began building right after that meeting. I went down the staff roster and started pulling math teachers, English teachers, social studies teachers, special education teachers, and so on—about 25 people altogether. I wanted classroom teachers' voices on the SIP team. I looked for the ones who were using the strategies I thought needed to be used, including engagement, authentic assessment, ongoing assessment, and differentiation of instruction. I didn't want to fill the team with yes-men and women. I wanted people who were going to stand up and have contrary opinions.

A week after that initial staff meeting, I had my first meeting with the 25 new SIP team members. When I opened the door, I can tell you it was the rowdiest, loudest group of people you ever saw. First, they broke into small groups by subject matter to figure out what the targets should be, then those groups broke down into strands—for example, measurement is always an issue in math. But I wanted them to break it down even further to look at the current SIP and decide what stays, what goes, what's real.

Create & Communicate Plan

I went with a coaching approach, but I didn't want them to get the feeling that I was looking down at them or telling them that they were wrong. Even Olympic athletes have coaches because there is always room for improvement. You have to balance it. For example, if they told me they were going to focus on informational text because that's low in our sixth grade," I said, "OK. Now what are we going to do after that, and how is the English—or math or social studies or science—teacher going to support that as well?" They had to keep coming back with more ideas.

They brought energy to the table and rewrote the SIP on the basis of those conversations. I kept telling them just to be honest, and they were; that was instrumental. When they sat together and looked at the SIP, it wasn't generalities anymore. It was targeting specific students with specific interventions that were based on our data. And the teachers were doing the targeting and strategizing. That was the buy-in.

Monitor & Adjust

After that, we presented the ideas to every staff member in every department. We talked to them about how the ideas stretched across the entire curriculum and involved everyone. The plan was where we needed to go as a team. They were conversing, and I realized they had not had that before. They were starting to see that I was serious when I said that it was our problem—not theirs, not mine—our problem. They were all open to it. We asked how can we best support their curricula? We had naysayers, but only one or two. For the most part the staff was really onboard with it. These were our kids. It became personal.

Create & Communicate Plan

Another goal of mine was to make the school a magnet school. The high school our students go on to requires them to have an accelerated English class, so I consulted my two eighth-grade English teachers about making our school a magnet school. Both teachers just looked at me. "Are you going to tell me right now that you don't have any students who can do accelerated English?" I asked. They said they might have a few. But I had already pulled the scores on the eighth graders, and I knew that 20% exceed standards, so together we started to go through the test score numbers. They were surprised at some of the students' scores, and we set a goal to create accelerated classes.

When that first piece was in place, I took a deep breath and thought, "You know, we have a shot. If I can get them this far—and then to the next piece—and really get them to understand how it translates back to their individual classrooms—we just might make it." What I was most afraid of was that it was all yes, yes, yes—but could we really do it!?

I called the district person on my SST team to tell him I was totally revamping the team. I explained the need to change in the best interests of the students and told him I wanted his support, but I wasn't going to take no for an answer. He asked if there was anything he could do.

Monitor & Adjust

I had him meet with my team, and they put it on the line, telling him how the current plan needed to change. First, we had to get the students out of double, triple reading programs. Schedules had to change. Then we talked to him about the bubble kids and the Sprint for the CRTs and how one of the intervention strategies for specific students was going to be a Saturday test-help program, the Cougar Camp.

The district provided someone to work with the staff as part of the Sprint for the CRTs initiative. We had morning and afternoon sessions for all teachers. I had 23 subs in the building one day! Before the district sent anyone, I told them the person couldn't come preach to my teachers because they wouldn't listen. They couldn't throw data at them because they would just zone out. Fortunately, they sent me the right person, and that got the staff talking. They had had conversations before, but never about application.

There was a lot of head nodding and a lot of "yeses" and then they started to make connections. Teachers were saying, "Well, I can do this in my classroom. Why can't I do that part for math as a review, if you tell me what terms I need to use for language arts…?" And, "You know, I have this really cool thing…" So that was the conversation back and forth. They broke up the information that needed to be taught so it was easier to swallow. And I stayed out of their training deliberately, only poking my head in a few times. A few complained about having to be out of their classrooms or missing their prep time, but only a few. For the most part, the staff was really onboard with the cross curriculum training.

Implement the Plan

The Saturday camps were successful. Turns out I was able to pay the teachers but they were committed anyway. They talked it up in their classrooms. The students even asked me in the hall, "Miss, if we are going to be there, are you going to be there?" I told them if they were there, I was going to be there.

The next step was to craft a letter inviting the students who were on the "bubble" of passing to participate. To get them to Saturday camp, we had to invite them personally. We called the students up to my office 15–20 at a time and talked to them about what it was and gave them a personalized letter of invitation. Out of 1,100 students, we invited about 600. We talked about their placement for the following year and told them that if they wanted to take electives, they had to test out well, so it was important. We told them to try their hardest. To emphasize the impact on their placement the following year, I told students that I was not going to sign a transcript that didn't show they were ready.

The invitation letter had to come back either way—and I told them I would hunt them down to stress how important it was for them to go. Keep in mind, there was no bus transportation; there was nothing I could do to force them to go to school on a Saturday. I gave them until Friday to have the letters back. That next Monday I went into classrooms and pulled students out into the hallway to ask them, "Where is my letter?"

They didn't think I was going to follow through. Once it got out that I wasn't playing, we got every single letter back.

During the first Saturday session, I remember that three sisters who usually barely made it to school came early. And because they were there, other students came as well. They didn't have to wear standard student attire—that was the deal-maker. The sisters came early to make sure I kept my word. The students also came because I told them there would be snacks. We also told them that if they were borderline with some of their grades, we would talk to their teachers if they came. For a lot of students, that was an important piece. And the cutest thing I remember, it almost broke my heart, is when one of the students came up to me and said, "Miss, thank you so much. I have never been to camp before." We made it something you had to be invited to. It became important to them and they really bought into it.

The camps also gave me a chance to speak with parents. Most of our parents are low-income and not legal and are afraid of the school, so I always got to the parking lot to talk to them, to thank them, and to ask about their children. It was like pulling teeth at first, but it got easier.

I set up an assembly for the Friday before the testing. We always have assemblies for sports and other activities—I wanted to do an academic assembly. I wanted them to understand how important the test was. They take tests all the time—more than I can count—and they're all important, but this one was *really* important.

With the SIP team members, I found some movie clips and interspersed teachers into them. There was a scene from *Armageddon* where they were all going to save the world; a scene from *Braveheart*; and a clip from *Friday Night Lights* when they are all sitting in the locker room talking about win or lose, you go out there and try your hardest. I needed the teachers to be part of it, because the students had relationships with those teachers. The cheerleaders performed. I talked to them about the importance of eating breakfast and told them, "Come here early. If you know a friend who is never here, make sure they are here."

A day before the test, I went to every room and talked to the students. "When you get a report card and you have to take it home and it has Fs all over it, how do you feel?" I asked, and they gave all the predictable answers. "My report card goes in the newspaper," I said. "It gets printed in the paper and everybody can see it. Last year my report said I had a big F. It was embarrassing. And I want to show everybody that we are not a bad school, so I need you guys to do a good job because we are not a bad school. Wouldn't you be proud if you got to open the newspaper and it said our school has an A?"

On test day, I focused on affect and environment. Teachers proctored for their own students. If I have strong teachers, I thought, the student is going to perform for them. I wanted as many teachers as possible to make the groups smaller. We pulled the ELL students and the IEP students who need smaller environments and made sure they were with the people most appropriate to test them. The logistics took some maneuvering on our part, but we did whatever was going to be best for the students.

To put a smile on their faces, we gave students "magic" pencils and wristbands with motivational slogans on them, such as "Intel Inside" and "I am Cool as a Cucumber." We gave out ice cream. I remember asking them what they wanted if we got the attendance we needed. Their big thing was a dress-down day. I told them we would have a dress-down day if we got 100% testing attendance. We did. There were kids I

Create & Communicate Plan

hadn't seen in several weeks who made sure they were there to test. I think their friends dragged them in because they wanted that dress-down day.

The test itself had two sections for every part: the bubbles students fill in and the constructed response questions. When all the tests were in, I went through them just to make sure there were no stray papers or anything. And on every test, every child had filled in the constructed response questions. That was something they hadn't done before. Even my ELL students who were new to the country had answered. They might not have been able to read it, but every child tried—and that was our goal. That effort almost brought tears to my eyes; they had tried their hardest. When we got the results several months later, we were all thrilled because scores had risen significantly—Cougar Camp and all of the other school efforts were a real success!

After that, the other pieces got easier.

Every piece of the SIP came together, but the SIP is worth nothing more than the paper on which it is written without transparency to the staff. After the test, I talked to them about how we had raised the bar for our students, and now we were going to keep raising the bar for ourselves. That philosophy was going to continue and grow and expand. My expectation was that we were going to be there for our students and bring our A game everyday.

Implement the Plan

Text-Based Discussion Questions

(See p. 35 for tips on leading a discussion)

1. One of the strategies that the principal used to gather data was to spend a day shadowing students. What would you expect to see if you were to shadow a student in your school for a day? How many different types of instructional strategies would be employed? What evidence would you need to see that would allow you to describe your school as "student-centered"?

2. This middle school had allocated many resources for intervention programs that were not working. What types of intervention strategies are in place at your school? Are they working? Do you have data to support your answer? Does your school focus on school improvement through the purchase of new curriculum or programs or do you focus on improving the skills of the people implementing the programs? What evidence supports your answer?

3. What strategies did the principal use to get the staff to buy in to large-scale school improvement efforts? How did she work with potential resistors to change? What has been done in your school to help the staff take ownership of the school's improvement efforts? On a scale of 1 to 10, where would you rate staff buy-in? What strategies does your school use to work with those resistant to change?

4. Managing, analyzing, and making sense of data played a crucial role in this school's effort to improve student performance. How does your school use data? Is it presented to teachers in a manageable, useful format? Do you have someone who is in charge of sharing accurate, accessible data with teachers so they can use it to inform instruction? Do you regularly overhear conversations among teachers that indicate that they understand and use data on a regular basis?

Chapter 3:
In Their Own Words:
Interviews with Two Principals

5. Although the principal's initial focus was to make changes that would result in improved student performance on state test scores, many of the changes necessitated creating a more personalized environment for the students. What examples of this did you note when reading this account? What efforts has your school made to make a more personalized environment for the students? What evidence can you provide to show that students in your school feel safe, respected, valued, and have a voice in their learning?

6. What impact did the school improvement efforts have on the culture of this school? How have the efforts to improve your student's performance affected your school culture? Would you say the effect has been positive? Why or why not? In three or four words, describe the culture of your school? Would other staff members agree with your assessment?

4 Gather and Analyze Data to Determine Priorities

It is a capital mistake to theorize before one has data.

—*Sir Arthur Conan Doyle*

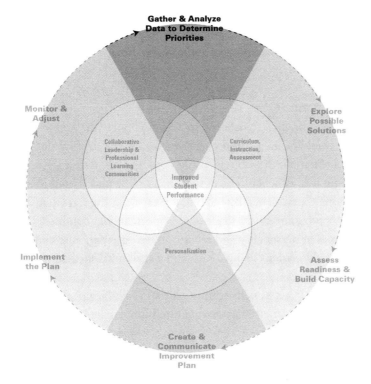

Good leaders are often good because they trust their intuition and use it to act quickly. It is difficult to put intuition on hold to take the time to identify and analyze data; however, **when contemplating changes in your school that affect culture and how you do business on a day-to-day basis, data-based decision making is the hallmark of success.**

An example of intuition run amok is when officials at one school system decided to improve the results on state exit exams by requiring any student who failed a state test in the eighth grade to take a special reading class. Sounds logical, right? Common sense would lead one to believe that students who failed those tests must have a reading problem.

Unfortunately, two years later, the same officials complained that the reading classes weren't working. If they had reviewed the data more carefully initially, they would have discovered that "only" half of the students who failed the state test actually had a reading problem. If they had asked the eighth-grade teachers, they would have quickly determined that the rest failed for a variety of reasons, mostly related to motivation and maturity. As a consequence of over-reliance on intuition and a cursory review of the data, half of each reading intervention class consisted of students who did not have a reading problem. Needless to say, discipline problems were rampant in those classes. A more careful analysis of the data would have indicated a need to address the personal needs of students in addition to a focus on a reading intervention. Think back to the interview of the high school principal in Chapter 3. The focused literacy program that was put into place at that school was coupled with strong connections between students and teachers.

There is another important reason for checking the facts before heading in a certain direction. Principals and teams who use intuition as a basis for starting a change effort are doomed to failure because the staff's first reaction will be, "That's his/her opinion." Since opinions are like noses—everybody has one—you don't want to unintentionally misdirect the focus away from a worthy initiative because the staff is caught up in personalities.

Diagnostic Assessment

- Don't rely on common sense…it isn't that common.
- Collect data and talk with the experts on the front lines to get their opinions.
- Never trust a single data point when making critical decisions about individuals or programs.

For example, when a principal transferred to a new school a few miles away, the staff assumed that she would begin a comprehensive literacy initiative similar to the one in her former school. After all, the schools, while not identical, were very similar demographically, and her former school was outperforming the new school in every category on state and national assessments. By making it clear from the start that she would not begin to plan a program until a diagnostic assessment was conducted, she was able to bypass the politics of personality and rely on facts. "After all," she said, "a doctor wouldn't treat a healthy patient or a patient who was ill until she had done a complete diagnosis."

While the diagnostic assessment confirmed that a significant portion of the students had serious reading deficiencies that required immediate intervention, waiting for those results instead of jumping right in from the start saved the school wasted time and effort. When the assessment results arrived, the literacy coach—not the principal— presented them to the staff. Neither the principal's opinion nor the principal's numbers led the staff to conclude that the students had reading problems. Instead of the staff challenging opinions, they asked, "What do we do?" Rather than providing a solution, the principal asked if anyone would be willing to become a part of a literacy council to discuss the results in-depth and begin to explore possible approaches.

Establish a Team to Review Data and Determine Priorities

Who will review and analyze the data? Who will develop possible solutions? Major change efforts require effective *Breaking Ranks* **teams**. In the example above, that team was the literacy council. The *BR* team is responsible for shepherding a specific change in culture and program within your school. *Breaking Ranks II* referred to these as *action planning teams*, but there are many other teams that schools have used based on their specific circumstances and the initiative or issues identified (e.g., instructional teams, literacy teams, numeracy teams, project teams). These teams are typically initiative-specific, whereas leadership teams, school improvement teams, and site councils look at the big picture and determine priorities based on the input of others. *BR* teams must be established to monitor the data, the process, and the implementation of *Breaking Ranks* recommendations. Often the *BR* team will have subteams that develop new strategies and try out new designs. (See "Skunkworks" on p. 68.) A detailed analysis of the action/initiative planning team and a discussion of selection and composition, level of experience, and many other resources may be found in *Breaking Ranks in the Middle* and *Breaking Ranks II.*

For the purposes of this guide we will refer to the initiative team as the *BR* team and refer to other teams (e.g., leadership team) as appropriate. Depending on the initiative, the *BR* team might be an existing team (e.g., a subgroup of the leadership team), a newly formed or existing team that includes teacher leaders or skill-specific staff members, students, parents, community leaders, or any combination that makes the most sense for bringing the initiative to fruition. The important thing is to put the right people on the bus in the right seats (Collins, 2001). Often, getting the right people on the team calls for *not* using existing groups with their related histories and other idiosyncrasies; however, it is critical to determine whether you have an existing structure or team that can accomplish the task. In some cases, it is better to add different or additional members to an existing team so that the new initiative doesn't feel like a new event or an additional time-drain. In addition, since the existing team already has processes and policies in place, less time can be spent on preliminary logistical and meeting groundwork.

The *BR* team must be able to recommend and execute well-developed communication and buy-in strategies, a focused data collection and analysis process, and appropriate professional development. As your team uses the *Breaking Ranks* Process Circle to guide your change process, keep in mind these caveats of change:

1. When newly formed or contemplating major changes, the team must establish trust and credibility with the staff before engaging in major change. (Of course, the team may not have the luxury of time if safety or security issues are in play or if you have specific mandates that must be addressed immediately.)

2. Most major change will take 12–24 months (sometimes as many as 36 months) to implement well and another year or two to fine tune and ensure it is self-sustaining. If you are being rushed, try to rearrange things to create more time. Barring that, do whatever you can to start small so that you can focus your efforts on doing what you can do well in the limited time available (get quick wins).

If your school has a negative change history, as most schools do in response to the many "programs du jour" they have endured over the years, count on the resistance to any major change to be high. You will have to do more than just paint a simple picture of the proposed benefits of the contemplated change. You will have to address the emotional side of the equation and plan how to engage everyone in the change process in a way that eliminates the past causes of failure. Be sure to build in enough time to deal with the negative change history and do whatever it takes to convince the majority of your staff through ongoing positive engagement that the proposed change will be done right and sustained over time.

Leaders gain trust when they take positions like the following:

- If it doesn't work, we will try something else.
- Time and methods are relative to the circumstances. Outcomes are absolute. We vary instructional time and differentiate instruction according to the needs of the individual students. Our goal is to help all students meet standards.

- It is not about being right or who gets the credit.
- We must concern ourselves with doing the right thing, the right way, for the right reasons.

Change Leadership Activities: Gather and Analyze Data to Determine Priorities

Many initiatives fail because teams don't take the time and effort necessary to get buy-in and clarify team member and stakeholder roles. The typical pattern is to identify a goal and then act immediately—which leads to failure in most cases. There are two general types of data (cultural and project/challenge specific) that can be used by two types of teams—leadership teams and *BR* teams. Each of these teams can use the Process Circle. For example, a principal or leadership team might choose to use interviews or other informal information or data to get the pulse of the culture and climate before they ever gathered data related to addressing specific areas of concern. They would then use that data—or work with a *BR* team—to determine priorities and explore possible solutions.

1. **Data about the culture of the school.** Data on school culture can provide valuable information on what is feasible. Use that information to sketch out an initial goal and a process for validating and meeting the goal. The main objective is to create the right focus for change and to start building support for that change. The valuable by-product of this data collection, when done with sensitivity and tact, is the building of trust and credibility. Some of the keys to success at this stage of the change process include:

- Treading softly—not beginning with preconceived ideas or pushing an agenda
- Listening—gathering both formal and informal data from multiple sources
- Identifying and speaking with staff members who will be candid and provide good data
- Establishing preliminary performance baselines
- Identifying causes for observed problems, e.g., identifying the reasons students are not performing up to par
- Building a preliminary case for change, including a cost-benefit analysis
- Identifying a preliminary change goal to address issues
- Identifying obstacles and potential sources of resistance
- Creating a preliminary change process roadmap
- Identifying potential resources and informal and formal change champions
- Evaluating the adequacy of current communication vehicles to support a major change effort.

Once your team gathers data related to culture, the *BR* team can proceed to gathering the data applicable to specific areas of change. This element of the change leadership process is crucial because the DNA of the project is established at this time. If team development, communication and buy-in, and data collection processes are not done correctly from the start, the project's chance of success is significantly compromised. The team must communicate the need for change in the most compelling way possible.

2. **Data about performance or a specific area of strength or challenge.** The *BR* team will likely take the lead on this and may work closely with the leadership team.

The questions in the following matrix delineate other items to consider as your team plans its activities around data.

Student Voice: An Oft-Overlooked Component

Just as students are often left out of discussions about their academic performance, so too are they sometimes neglected when it comes to issues of school climate, the curriculum, and a host of other issues that directly affect them. In so many instances, the bus schedule or the needs of adults dictate what happens to students—those silent partners in the educational process who legally have very little choice but to attend to whatever adults say they must, regardless of the quality. (Visit www.principals.org to download surveys to aid you in garnering support for your school initiatives.)

Leadership teams must develop methods to find out what students are thinking and what their interests are. In addition to personal learning plans and advisories and student membership on leadership teams or school boards, consider Raising Student Voice and Participation (RSVP), a initiative of NASSP's National Association of Student Councils that helps schools encourage students to be partners in the school change process. RSVP will enable leadership teams to understand the school, community, and global issues that most concern students. RSVP also:

- Provides principals with a way to utilize the leadership of their student councils to engage students more and personalize their school experience

- Involves every student and all student populations, specifically giving those students who are typically not involved an opportunity to share their voices and participate in civic-based activities

- Establishes a process and framework for developing and implementing student-directed projects

- Brings abstract learning to life.

The leadership team can address specific concerns revealed by the data students compile. The "simple" act of giving every student a voice—the goal of RSVP—is in and of itself a step toward changing the culture of the school. (Visit www.nasc.us/rsvp.)

Activities: Gather and Analyze Data to Determine Priorities

The following matrix reflects those core change leadership elements and questions that surface during the data gathering stage of the change process. Each section of the process circle has a similar matrix. *(The list below is a sample and is not intended to provide all of the information for any given initiative. Tailor it to your school's needs.)* The *BR* team should discuss and complete the activities matrix in each chapter. This exercise will help to ensure that your team has considered most areas related to the initiative. A sample of what a "combined" activity chart might look like can be found in the last section "Tying It All Together."

Essential Elements of Each Step	**Sources of Data and Analysis**	■ See *Breaking Ranks II*, pp. 26–31 and *Breaking Ranks in the Middle*, pp. 63–65. ■ Establish and implement a formal data collection and analysis process. Often a subteam will conduct research and work with the school or district data team to obtain the required information. ■ Identify disaggregated student outcome data to establish performance baselines. You may discover during this process that essential learnings have not been adequately established, which may become one of your major change goals. (See *Breaking Ranks II*, pp. 6–8 and *Breaking Ranks in the Middle*, pp. 8–10) ■ Evaluate classroom practices. ■ Employ activities to collect the voice of the student and the voice of the parent.
	Collaborative Leadership	■ Is decision making distributed appropriately across key stakeholders? ■ Are meaningful tasks delegated both for implementation and development purposes? ■ How can the selection of the initial team members reinforce collaborative leadership? ■ What is the composition of the team? Are all key stakeholder groups represented? Are students on the team? ■ Are students being given a leadership role in gathering data? ■ Are students taking a leading role in obtaining data from their peers? ■ Are students taking a leading role in presenting data to the team or other stakeholder groups? ■ What is the principal's role in this change effort? ■ Should the principal be part of the team? If so, in what role? ■ Does the team have the authority to set final goals and to implement them? ■ What approvals are needed from supervisors to move forward on the goals selected? ■ What leadership support is required from the district to ensure success?
	Infrastructure Capacity	■ Do systems, policies, and procedures help or hinder getting work done? ■ Are resources allocated fairly and reasonably? ■ What system improvements will be necessary to support a major change initiative? ■ Do we need to set up any new systems to track relevant data? If so, do we have sufficient resources to do so? ■ Are sufficient resources available to support the team and overall change effort? If not, what must be done to obtain them?

Activities: Gather and Analyze Data to Determine Priorities

Worksheet

(Note: An electronic version of this worksheet is available at www.principals.org/brguide)

Essential Elements of Each Step — **Sources of Data and Analysis**	
Collaborative Leadership	
Infrastructure Capacity	

Communication and Buy-in	■ Have you: • Identified and prioritized stakeholders and their needs when it comes to communication and potential resistance to proposed goals • Created and implemented an effective communication and buy-in plan based on your stakeholder analysis • Created new communication vehicles (or used existing) to support the communication and buy-in plan? • Incorporated the case for change into the communication and buy-in plan ■ Are communications adequate? ■ To what degree is the leadership team or *BR* team communicating appropriate expectations and providing encouragement for meeting our vision and mission? ■ To what degree do members of the team model the values that are essential for success as an organization? ■ How is the team viewed? ■ Is the current level of trust and credibility sufficient to drive a major change initiative? ■ If not, what needs to be done to strengthen how the change is viewed by others? ■ To what degree have people bought into the need for change? ■ Who are the stakeholders who will be most affected by the goals? ■ Which stakeholders are likely to oppose the proposed changes? ■ Who will own the communication and buy-in process for this project? An individual on the team? Or a subteam of the project team? ■ What must be done to ensure that key stakeholders are brought on board? ■ Have potential resistors been assigned to the project team or involved in the project in some way?
Professional Development	■ Is the staff receiving sufficient professional development to meet current goals? ■ What professional development might be necessary if a major change initiative were undertaken? ■ Who should be on the project team for development purposes? ■ What type of training does the team need to be effective in managing the change process, with regard to data collection and analysis, communication and buy-in strategies, and the goal selected? (e.g., if a personalization goal such as establishing an advisory program were selected, what training and technical assistance would be required?)

Essential Elements of Each Step

Activities: Gather and Analyze Data to Determine Priorities

Worksheet

(Note: An electronic version of this worksheet is available at www.principals.org/brguide)

Essential Elements of Each Step	Communication and Buy-in	
	Professional Development	

Case Study: A Shaky Start

The following example provides evidence of what happens when the team development, communication and buy-in, and data collection and analysis processes have not been adequately addressed at this point in the change process.

When I became principal of a large suburban high school, I was keenly aware of a number of things:

- The school would be growing rapidly over the next few years as the result of a boundary change and new home construction.
- A new addition to the building (22 classrooms) would be added during a two-year, construction project.
- The long-established community was experiencing a marked influx of English language learners.
- The number of students eligible for free and reduced-price meals was growing—not only because of the boundary change or the ELL growth—although that was part of the perception.
- By my second or third year as principal, the 9th grade would be approximately twice the size of the 12th grade.
- Ninth-grade promotion rates were low.
- Some staff members still clung to the idea that if 9th grade were moved back to "junior high, where it belonged," things would be better.

The data showed a number of areas for improvement, but the 9th-grade data pointed to some glaring issues. Many 9th graders were being retained each year and all indications were that those numbers would continue to grow. Some teachers did not want to teach ninth graders and the common refrain was that the middle schools were not preparing the students well. The leadership team talked about potential approaches to the problem, including:

- Improving articulation with the middle schools
- Instituting a study skills program for all 9th graders
- Designating a grade level administrator for the 9th grade
- Implementing teams at the 9th-grade level.

The leadership team included the heads of all of the departments (English, social studies, mathematics, science, foreign language, business education, physical education, career and technical education, guidance, English for speakers of other languages, and special education), the three assistant principals, and the coordinator of a special education program for students with emotional disabilities. Without belaboring the point, I'll say that consensus was nearly impossible. There were almost as many agendas as group members. Even though we seemed to agree that we had to do something to address the ninth-grade problem, we all saw the possible approaches differently. Of course, that led to very long and contentious meetings, many compromises, and ultimately the failure of a major part of the initiative—the ninth-grade team.

The initiative didn't fail because it wasn't needed—we didn't get the "what" wrong. We needed to address the low ninth-grade promotion rate. We got the "how" wrong... we failed to practice what we knew about positive, focused school change. So what happened and what didn't happen?

- We improved the quality of and the approach to our meetings with the staffs at the feeder middle schools, redefined the type of data that we needed from them, and changed the time of year that we began transition conversations with the middle schools. But only one of the two middle schools cooperated. The school that sent us about one-third of their eighth-grade students told us, with no room for compromise, that they were unwilling to do something different with us than they did with the other high school where they sent two-thirds of their eighth graders. We proceeded to make changes with the cooperative middle school, but we were aware that some of the ninth graders who were at risk came from the "uncooperative" middle school.

- We adopted a study skills program, but we later learned that not all teachers did what they said they would do to make the program work. We didn't get the buy-in that we thought we had.

- The assistant principal who volunteered to be the ninth-grade administrator started the school year very strong, but at mid-year, problems caused his follow-through to become an issue that didn't become apparent for quite some time.

- The leadership team could not agree on the implementation of ninth-grade teams, so as a compromise we implemented only a single team (English, math, social studies and science) for ninth graders whose profiles indicated that they might be at risk for failing.

- The school was overcrowded, so we had to use a number of portable classrooms. Because of previous commitments the arrangement was not ideal—English, social studies, and math were outside and quite a distance from other members of their departments. The science teacher was inside because the lab was needed for the class, so not only was the team not connected to their subject-area peers but they were also not together as a team.

- We didn't get them the support they needed to learn to work as a team, which we didn't recognize until the end of the first quarter. Through no fault of their own, they didn't know how to work as a team.

- The team lacked strong connections to their students, although they were connected to some students and certainly willing to do what was needed to help students.

A Critique

Our goal was to provide support to the ninth graders who were most at risk without disrupting what worked pretty well for many of the students. We made the error of "tinkering abound the edges." Rather than being audacious in our change initiative, we chose to take small steps. Ted Sizer (2002) wrote, "You have to change enough fast enough so that gravity does not pull you back." We took steps that turned out to be too small. We went with one ninth-grade team when all of the ninth grade would have benefited from a focused team approach.

Despite the best of intentions we put the needs/desires of the adults in the building ahead of the needs of the students. We located the ninth-grade team in portable classrooms so that the teachers would have proximity to one another and interact across disciplines. We didn't anticipate the unintended consequence of the team members being cut off from their departments. The one exception was the science teacher who of course needed to be located in a lab. This problem relates to the next—and the one I think was my greatest error in judgment. All of the teachers on the team were in their first three years of teaching! They did not know how to be a team and we did not teach them. We focused on the "what" again—not the "how." We failed to provide them with the professional development they needed to learn the "how" of teaming. They were young and inexperienced, so they naturally focused their own efforts on becoming better at teaching their subject matter. They were at times overwhelmed by the needs of their students.

Eventually, I made the decision that if they focused on their subject matter and spent less time on the teaming activities, more would be accomplished for the students. In the end they became better teachers, but we still had too many students who were not making it. I wish I could do this over again—I'd be much better prepared to focus on the "how."

Change Leadership Tools: Gather and Analyze Data to Determine Priorities

On the following pages are tools and other materials that will assist you during this phase of the change process:

- General Questions for Your Team to Consider That May Require Data
- *Breaking Ranks* Team Staffing Protocol
- How Well Does Your School Serve Each Student Survey Instrument
- School Culture Evaluation Exercise
- Interview/Focus Group Protocol

Note: Due to various circumstances at individual schools, the tools are not necessarily provided in the order in which a team would use or administer them. In addition, it is likely that not every tool is appropriate for every school. Additional tools that can be conveniently completed online are available at www.principals.org.

General Questions for Your Team to Consider That May Require Data

These questions will help you review the data more carefully and systematically.

- Is the culture truly student centered?
- Are good student and classroom practice data available?
- Are the data disaggregated?
- Are the data of sufficient quality and quantity to make good decisions?
- Are teams structured appropriately and are they performing well?
- What data is available regarding the extent to which staff members freely share information and practices?
- Is the staff performing at a high level as reflected by student outcomes?
- Is the workload reasonable and distributed equitably?
- Is the climate positive? (What data support this?)
- What is the school's change history?
- Who are the champions of change?
- Who can be trusted to provide good information?
- What are the sources of resistance to change?
- What resources are available to conduct a successful change process?
- What are the primary needs and issues?
- Does it make more sense to start small or to start big?
- What relevant data is available concerning the issues and goals we are addressing?
- If the data isn't available, i.e., the quality and quantity is not sufficient for good decision making, what must be done to obtain it?
- Given the level of effort required, do we need a research/data subteam of the project team to do the work?
- What methodologies can we employ to understand the voice of the student, e.g., student shadowing, student interviews and focus groups, student visioning exercises?
- Have we reviewed the *BR* recommendations to assure that we are addressing the three core areas?

Breaking Ranks **Team Staffing Protocol**

This tool can be used by the principal or leadership team to do the initial staffing of the team and/or by the *BR* team to ensure that the team has appropriate stakeholder representation and the appropriate people on subteams.

1. List the type of stakeholders needing representation on the team:

2. List the potential team roles:

CURRENT POSITION	NAME	TEAM PLAYER (Low/Med/ High)	CONTENT EXPERT (Low/Med/ High)	POLITICAL BUY-IN (Low/Med/ High)	COMMIT. TO GOAL (Low/Med/ High)	TIME REQ'D HRS/WK	TIME AVAIL HRS/WK	POTENTIAL TEAM ROLE

How Well Does Your School Serve Each Student?

Use this survey with your team and staff members to assess their perception of school staff in meeting the needs of each student consistent with *Breaking Ranks* recommendations.

Please write your answer/observation and then rate your degree of satisfaction with the current status. (5 = extremely satisfied; 4= very satisfied; 3= satisfied; 4= dissatisfied; 5= very dissatisfied)

Question	Answer/Observations	Degree of Satisfaction
1. Do the instructional teams and departments in your school regularly use data to assess their effectiveness in planning and delivering challenging and developmentally appropriate lessons?		
2. What percentage of your students are achieving at a proficient or higher level of performance and are promoted "on time"?		
3. What percentage of your students say they are well known by at least one adult in the building who knows their aspirations, strengths, and weaknesses and helps them become successful?		
4. How much time is *scheduled* each week for teachers to collaborate on planning instruction, reviewing student work, aligning instructional units with standards, and encouraging interdisciplinary learning?		
5. What percentage of classroom instruction relies on active, project-based inquiry rather than lecture?		
6. What percentage of your students participate in school programs or services that link to real life applications and to college awareness and planning?		
7. What percentage of students avail themselves of the opportunity to give input and feedback into the academic and social activities and programs at your school?		
8. What percentage of the school's teachers say they have received adequate professional development *and* the time to collectively and regularly assess student data and plan for curriculum integration?		
9. What percentage of your students are involved in ongoing programs that develop skills in decision making, core values, conflict resolution, self awareness, respect, and stress management?		

Question	Answer/Observations	Degree of Satisfaction
10. How well do staff members interact with all parents—especially those who are hard to reach?		
11. What percentage of the teachers, students, and parents surveyed indicate that the transition into and out of your school is effective and appropriate?		
12. What percentage of your graduates must take remedial courses or other recovery programs as they matriculate to high school or college?		
13. What percentage of each student's classroom assessment is authentic (e.g. portfolio reviews, student-led presentations, student projects) and what percentage is traditional standardized tests?		
14. To what extent is enrollment in advanced or gifted and talented courses reflective of the school's demographics?		
15. What percentage of your students are involved in ongoing programs that develop skills in critical thinking, problem solving, organization and study methods, and formal and informal communications?		

School Culture Evaluation Exercise

The opposite page contains a list of cultural elements that characterize school philosophies and practices. The left column reflects a culture that is not conducive to enhancing student outcomes, and the right column reflects cultural elements that research has validated as supporting personalization and improved student outcomes. An accurate depiction of your culture will provide you with a sense of the level of effort and time it will take to implement your proposed change goal.

Purpose:

- To provide a picture of your school's current culture
- To provide a picture of the culture required to support your proposed *Breaking Ranks* changes
- To highlight the cultural gaps that must be addressed prior to the changes being implemented or addressed in parallel with the changes
- To foster a discussion among team members and stakeholders that clarifies what best practices are required for positive change—to get people on the same page
- To provide stakeholders with an idea of the scope of proposed changes and the level of effort and time required to plan for and implement the change.

Who: The *Breaking Ranks* team and other stakeholders as appropriate to support project goals and approach.

When: At the beginning of the change leadership process, i.e., once data has been collected and options identified and prior to capacity assessment and building.

How Long: 40–60 minutes.

How:

- As a group:
  - Reach consensus on a definition for each word or phrase before the group rates it.
  - Place a "C" on each arrow to reflect where your school currently stands on each culture element. Take time to discuss different perspectives and work to come to a consensus placement.
  - Mark F on each arrow to reflect where your school needs to be in the future to adequately support your goals. Take time to discuss different perspectives and work to come to a consensus placement.
- As individuals:
  - Prior to starting the exercise, recreate the form on a flipchart or board.
  - Ask each person to fill out the form on their own. Provide definitions of words or phrases as required.
  - When each person has filled out the form, ask them to replicate their results on the flipchart or board.
  - As above, go through the results and come to a consensus on what the words and phrases mean and where the Cs and Fs go.

Processing the Results: When done as individuals, note first the disparity of perspectives and the implications for getting everyone to agree. Identify large and noteworthy C–F gaps and discuss the implications for your goals. Identify actions that must be taken on the basis of your analysis, i.e., what it will take to turn Cs into Fs. Use this survey with your team to ascertain the status of school culture as it relates to student performance. Discuss areas of perceived weakness in depth.

School Culture Evaluation Exercise

Instructions:

■ Place a C on each arrow to reflect where your school currently stands on each culture element listed.

■ Place an F on each arrow to show where your school needs to be in the future to adequately support your proposed change goal.

■ The school culture is focused on the needs of the adults in the building	⟶	■ The school culture is focused on what is best for the students
■ What is being taught is most important	⟶	■ What is being learned is most important
■ The emphasis is on covering the subject matter content	⟶	■ The emphasis is on students demonstrating mastery of content
■ Teachers tend to "close their door" and teach in isolation	⟶	■ Teachers work together in collaborative teams
■ Teachers rarely interact with one another regarding professional practices	⟶	■ Sharing of professional practices happens on a regular basis
■ Assessments are rarely given, summative in nature, and tend to be tests used to reward and punish student performance	⟶	■ Assessments are frequent, balanced, formative in nature, and used to inform instruction
■ Common assessments have not been developed	⟶	■ Common assessments are regularly used in all core content areas
■ Support programs are designed to remediate learning	⟶	■ Support programs are designed to intervene for successful learning
■ The staff isolates the students into "your kids and my kids"	⟶	■ The staff embraces the students as "our kids"
■ Professional development efforts are not focused on school improvement goals	⟶	■ Professional development is individualized, on-going, job-embedded, and designed to aid in school improvement efforts
■ Grading policies are punitive in nature and discourage students	⟶	■ Grading policies enhance student motivation and encourage students to never give up

Interview or Focus Group Protocol

This tool provides you with a qualitative data-gathering strategy for obtaining information from individuals or groups. It is intended to foster conversation rather than to be used like a survey with content-specific items.

- This tool should be modified to fit your situation. Tailor the probes to fit the stakeholder with whom you are speaking. There are more probes than anyone will typically need. Identify those that best meet your needs and the people you are interviewing.

- As a general technique, if someone expresses a concern or complaint, push for data and ask for examples. Also push for data to support positive responses.

Explain the Purpose of the Interview/Meeting

- To gather data to understand stakeholder needs

- To gather data to understand what's working and what could be improved

- To gather data to understand current initiatives

- To gather data to support implementation of a specific initiative

Explain Confidentiality

- Data won't be shared with anyone

- Data will only be shared as theme—there will be no attribution of data to any specific person

Interview Strategy

- Use the probes as a starting point for discussion

- Select the questions that best meet your needs

- Follow the probes with requests for more detail and information

Sample Probes—Broad

■ What's working?

■ What's not working?

■ What would you like to see more of?

■ What would you like to see less of?

■ What prevents you from…?

■ How would you describe the climate here?

■ Since you've been here, what major change efforts have made the most difference. Why?

■ If you remember change efforts that did not succeed, what were the reasons they didn't meet expectations?

■ If you remember change efforts that succeeded, why did they succeed?

■ What are the major challenges for you? for students? for teachers? for administrators? for support staff?

■ Since you've been here, what's changed for the better?

■ Since you've been here, what's changed for the worse?

Sample Probes—Focused

■ What is the school's vision/mission/values?

■ How would you describe communications here?

■ To what degree are parents involved?

■ To what degree is the community involved?

■ What's the first word that comes to mind when you think of this school?

■ What supports are you receiving that assist you in your job?

■ What is professional development like here?

■ What are the school's primary goals?

■ What do people at this school value most?

■ What is your school's biggest strength?

■ What is your school's biggest limitation?

■ What is the best experience you've ever had here?

■ What is the worst experience you've ever had here?

■ If you could change one thing, what would it be?

■ How helpful is the district office?

Other Probes—Add Your Own:

■

Challenges and Tips:
Developing the Team's Capacity to Gather and Prioritize

- A team must have clear authority to make decisions and to act. It is the engine of change.

- Do whatever it takes early in the team's life to define what commitment to the team means and to ensure that all the members are on board with that level of commitment. If the team stutters, the change process stutters.

- If you want true commitment, help team members take something off their plates so they can focus on their role as a team member. Review all the responsibilities, work demands, and initiatives that exist in the school and reprioritize them or compensate team members for their time.

- Clearly define roles, responsibilities, and duties (roles can be developed by the team). Typical roles on a major change project team or subteam include team leader, facilitator, recorder, program content expert, and a point person on communication and buy-in and another on research/data.

Characteristics to Look for in Potential Team Members

- A commitment to growth and development
- A reputation for innovation
- An ability to make things happen
- Evidence of energy and persistence
- Demonstrated leadership ability
- A willingness to work
- Patience
- The respect of the faculty
- Small and large group communication skills (Painter, Lucas, Wooderson, & Valentine, 2000, p. 4).

Early Warning Signs of Teams in Trouble

- Team members cannot easily describe or agree on the team's purpose.
- Meetings are formal, stuffy, or tense.
- Broad participation produces minimal accomplishment.
- There is talk, but not much communication.
- Team members air disagreements privately after meetings.
- The leader makes all decisions.
- Members are confused or disagree about roles or work assignments.
- Key people outside the team are not cooperative.
- The team does not assess its progress or processes (p. 8).

Communication and Buy-In

- Prepare to embrace the resistance that is generated. Keep in mind that **if there is no real resistance, there is no real change.**

- Conduct a thorough stakeholder analysis. Resistance can come from any quarter. Don't be blindsided by thinking that the only resistance will come from your staff members and parents; it is not uncommon to get resistance from the district office as well.

- The antidote to resistance is a well–thought out and executed communication and buy-in plan that covers every aspect of the project, including how data is collected from and presented to stakeholders. Remember that mastering the technical side (e.g., program content knowledge) of any change is the easy part. It is the people side that takes most of the time and energy.

- Follow a well-defined meeting protocol that includes guidelines for determining what is to be communicated. (You want to be sure everyone is reading from the same page.) Release information in a timely manner, but not prematurely. At the early stages of a project, it is fine to describe what the team is doing in very broad terms, (e.g., We are engaged in a process to find out what we should do to assist our students with literacy. As soon as we have specific ideas, we will share them with everyone for their input.)

- To be successful you must turn most of your resistors into advocates. This takes time and engagement by your *BR* team members (and the leadership team) who are the ambassadors of change. Part of this influence process is accomplished by creating a data-based case for change that is presented in a fashion to win people over.

- Don't be surprised if most people don't embrace your goals and jump on the change bandwagon, regardless of how compelling a picture you draw of the benefits. It's not human nature to embrace change, particularly if your school has a negative change history, (i.e., many change efforts have gone by the wayside with little if any impact—other than a perceived waste of time and effort). Typically, a very small percentage of your population will be early adopters of change, a large majority will play the wait-and-see game, and the remainder will never embrace what you are trying to do regardless of what you do.

- Because of the human element, it takes 12–24 months (or sometimes as many as 36 months) to get any major change implemented, and then another year or two to make adjustments and sustain it. Many programs fail because of an imposed implementation time limit that is far too short, (e.g., 3–4 months is not unusual; in June everyone is told a new program will be started in September).

- A formal communication process must start with the first action team meeting.

Data Collection and Analysis

- Devote significant time to amassing good data to support your goal setting (a subteam often does the data collection and analysis work).

- Obtain qualitative data as well as quantitative data and capture information from all your key stakeholders, *including* students and parents. A well-executed data-collection strategy has the secondary benefit of promoting communication and gaining buy-in.

- Data collection and analysis will provide information that will allow you to set specific student outcome goals; however, setting goals in terms of the approaches to be employed to meet your student outcome goals will take more effort and is addressed in the next chapter.

It is worth repeating the types of data to consider:

- *Demographic data:* Ethnic population, mobility rate, poverty indicators, parents' education, housing, etc.

- *Academic data:* State test scores, other testing data (SAT, ACT, PSAT, etc), district, school, and/or classroom assessments, failure rates, interim progress reports, observations of classroom practice—what's actually happening in the classroom, etc.

- *Diagnostic assessment data:* Reading, writing, mathematics (RTI)

- Behavioral data: Attendance, suspensions, referrals, expulsions, interventions, counselor visits, bullying issues, harassment

- *Miscellaneous data:* NASSP's satisfaction surveys (staff, parent, students—visit www.principals.org), surveys of business/community, exit interviews/surveys, etc.

- *Student perception data:* Student shadowing, student forums (e.g., NASSP's Raising Student Voice and Participation (RSVP) model.

Sort the data by subgroups; look for patterns, growth, and declines over time; correlations across subjects; equity of access to challenging classes; etc.

5 Explore Possible Solutions

Impossible only means that you haven't found the solution yet.

—*Anonymous*

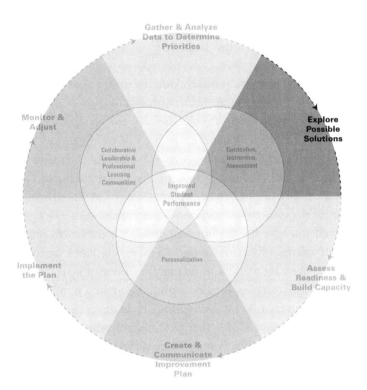

You've scanned your environment, pulled a *Breaking Ranks* (*BR*) team together, delved into the data, identified the issues, and established some preliminary goals. If you are action oriented, a successful trait of most school leaders, the temptation to grab a solution and head to the races is almost too powerful to overcome. But overcome it you must! The following story from a school improvement coach illustrates why:

> I can't tell you how hard it is to slow people down once the goals and apparent solutions seem clear. Intellectually, everyone gets the "go slow to go fast" concept—the need to plan well, to investigate approaches, and to spend time communicating and creating buy-in. But left to their own devices, most won't do it. They will jump from preliminary data collection right to implementation, bypassing a number of key activities such as a thorough investigation of solutions, testing their readiness, creating buy-in, and building capacity to manage the change process. Let me give you a recent example.

I was running a three-day summer workshop on the design and development of student-led conferences. Whenever I do workshops, I introduce key change leadership concepts at different points in the program. It was obvious that my presentation of those concepts had made an impact, because three of the six school teams in the workshop decided to delay their program implementation by 6–12 months. That was not an easy decision; all three teams knew they would get significant push-back from either their fellow teachers or the principal who had promised the district office that the program would be started in the fall. However, they realized the value of going through the change leadership process and wanted to ensure that their student-led conference program would not have the same sad fate as earlier initiatives—quick off the blocks, quick fade, and failure to cross the finish line.

What was particularly interesting was that on the morning of the third day, I saw a new person in the workshop sitting with one of the teams. He was in an animated discussion with three team members. At the break, I went over to the group to see if I could get a handle on what was going on. As I got close, he jumped up to meet me. He had a look of concern on his face, and before I could say a word he said, "I didn't sign up for your program (he had been in a different workshop) but I had to talk to my team to convince them not to delay the start of the student-led conference program at our school. I'm the team leader, and you have no idea how important it is to get this program off the ground immediately. Everyone in our school expects it! However, my team is telling me we have a lot of work to do first, and I don't buy it!" His team members, obviously frustrated, pleaded with him to take a minute to listen to me. I started the conversation by asking him, "How many new initiatives have you tried in the last five years?" He thought for a moment and said, "At least a half-dozen." I then asked, "How many were successful?" He thought for a moment and then replied, "None." The point being made, I spent a couple minutes reinforcing what his team had told him, and he accepted their decision to put the program on hold for at least six months.

Will your team be able to control the impulse to rush or take the time to do a thorough investigation of which approach will best address your issues and meet your goals and ultimately turn that approach into a compelling change vision for your school? The following section will describe a low-risk, high-yield team approach that can help make sure that your school doesn't rush into an initiative before its time.

Skunkworks

The *BR* team will likely have subgroups working on specific areas, troubleshooting, innovating, and experimenting. One of those subgroups might be a skunkworks.

Skunkworks is a fast-moving project- or program-focused team of educators working within the structure of the school but free of the normal restrictions. The laser-like focus and voluntary nature of these efforts allows staff members to work in relative privacy and obscurity free from the normal skepticism and criticism. Taken from the name of the moonshine distillery in the *Li'l Abner* cartoon strip, skunkworks initiatives take the focus away from the individual "star performer" and promote teamwork and collaboration among staff members.

Working together to solve mission-specific challenges, skunkworks teams consist of six to eight core members, usually teachers, working with a support team led by the principal and other professionals with specific areas of expertise related to the project. The core team may be homogenous in nature (consisting, for instance, entirely of Algebra I teachers working on improving student Algebra performance) or a heterogeneous group made up of teachers from a number of subject areas and departments focusing on a schoolwide initiative such as literacy or technology integration. The team is given autonomy, resources, and technical assistance.

A mainstay strategy of the corporate world since its development by Lockheed Martin in 1943, skunkworks speaks to principals who want to jumpstart a change in school culture. This strategy minimizes pushback and creates "quick wins" (not quick *fixes*) while removing the risk of failure that often accompanies a large scale, schoolwide effort. A skunkworks is fast-moving yet does not interfere with other efforts and does not pose a threat to the existing organizational structures. In any secondary school, it would not be uncommon to find two or more skunkworks projects occurring at once.

The skunkworks core team collaborates informally and frequently. The entire skunkworks team—core and support—meets regularly. The team members discuss what works as well as the problems that they are experiencing, and they identify additional resources they need and next steps. The role of the support team is to remove barriers—ask clarifying questions, identify the desired state, locate and test possible solutions, and secure necessary resources prior to the next meeting. Considered "notoriously pragmatic" (Peters & Waterman, 2004, p. 212), a skunkworks is about changing the culture of the school. Although the initial focus of the project is limited in scope, the process is transformational—designed to change the way people work, interact, and think by:

- Fostering collaboration and teamwork
- Redistributing leadership
- Promoting emergent leadership
- Changing the focus of the staff from everyday problems to solutions
- Fostering learning by doing, continuous growth, and improvement
- Motivating the staff
- Creating organizational momentum.

This strategy should not be confused with pilot programs. Pilot programs are typically driven by a mandate of "take this, use it, and make it work" and usually take on a life of their own. And they don't die. After all, once given a resource in a resource-scarce environment, resourceful leaders are reluctant to give it up. Give a principal a hammer, and any problem can be made to look like a nail. Yet. what principals really need is a project-focused strategy *designed to find solutions* to a real problem in their school—not be given a tool and told to find a problem for the tool to solve.

"The essence of mastering systems thinking as a management discipline lies in seeing patterns where others see only events and forces to react to."

—Peter Senge, *The Fifth Discipline: The Art and Practice of the Learning Organization*

Chapter 5:
Explore Possible Solutions

Anatomy of a Change Effort

An Interview with John O'Neill, Principal of Forest Grove (OR) High School, a 2008 MetLife Foundation–NASSP Breakthrough School

When John O'Neill was appointed principal of Forest Grove High School, he knew he faced challenges and significant pressure to implement changes. Available data and a survey of students and the community that had been commissioned by the superintendent provided some insights: Students felt the school environment was impersonal; student achievement was lacking; and the school had the highest drop-out rate in the county (7.7%) and a low graduation rate.

Q: What process did you use to identify possible solutions for improvement?

I used a schoolwide examination of *What Works In Schools* by Robert Marzano along with student achievement data to mobilize the call to action. We had received a smaller learning communities planning grant from the U.S. Department of Education and we used this to investigate promising practices, make site visits, offer staff development opportunities, and conduct a spring school-improvement retreat that affected all stakeholders. During the retreat, we examined school and teacher factors that impact student achievement. As a result of the retreat, we agreed to:

- Pursue a smaller learning communities implementation grant ($500,000, which we received that summer)
- Implement a links transition program
- Implement teams or houses at the ninth- and tenth-grade levels (social studies, English, and science teachers with a common prep period sharing a common group of students)
- Implement career academies at the 11th and 12th grades
- Implement reading and math workshops at the ninth- and tenth-grade levels for any student in danger of not passing the state assessment by the end of 10th grade
- Refine and expand our AP program
- Improve communication with parents about student progress (EdLine as a result)
- Expand and refine our alternative program.

Q. When you say "we"—who was involved in making the decision to pursue these?

All stakeholders were present, which included representation from students, parents, local school committee/building site council members, school board members, district office administrators, all school departments, classified representatives, and all site administrators. Further, all program managers were brought in as part of the program review process that identified program structure, successes, and challenges and then identified next steps for the succeeding three to five years. As a result, achievement data was reviewed, feedback received, discussions held, and goals set for all programs. These coalesced into schoolwide goals for the next three to five years and had a direct impact on our schoolwide professional development efforts. These representatives, when questioned as to why changes were occurring and what those changes were, were able to speak with one voice and with conviction. We also agreed to reconvene every other spring to ensure that we're on track to meet student needs.

Q: How did you determine if the school was ready for change?

School performance data was our call to action. My first year we received negative press on having the highest drop-out rate in the county and one of the lowest achievement rates in reading and math. By using a rotating staff meeting during teacher prep periods, we examined the school-level and teacher-level factors that play a part in student achievement, the two factors on which we have the greatest impact. We used this review in smaller settings with cross-sections of our staff members to highlight the need for improvement.

Q: What strategies did you use to ensure the change had the best chance of succeeding?

First, we needed to get away from the grind of the daily life of high school to have uninterrupted time to have these frank discussions. We tried to do it during our leadership team meetings, in staff meetings, after school, etc.—but all we would do was get into storming and then run out of time. People would leave angry or concerned that change was pending and worried about their programs. We had to bring the data and research together along with all stakeholder representatives so that we could get past storming and get into norming.

You also need to have a skilled administrative site team to know when to proceed and when to wait because all of the necessary changes can't all take place at one time. They need to be integrated over the school year during the planning year. Then, you need to be flexible where you can be flexible to ensure student success is maintained and continuous improvement is supported.

Lastly, a great deal of communication. We had quarterly newsletters written in English and Spanish, the school Web site, board presentations, staff meetings, parent meetings, presentations at the feeder middle school by the principal to students and then parents, and the biannual school improvement retreat.

Q: How do you evaluate success and monitor and adjust the process when needed?

We created a classified position of an assessment coordinator who oversees all online state assessments, worksample data, and site-level formative assessments. This person is also responsible for providing data notebooks in which reading, math, and writing scores are provided to all teachers and updated each semester on a class-by-class, student-by-student basis. Various committees and program administrators provide periodic updates to our school's leadership team and comprehensive reviews are held every other year at our school improvement retreats and necessary adjustments are made accordingly.

Q: What has enabled your school to sustain the changes made?

Constant tracking of individual student progress by the school principal, program leaders, and workshop teachers through a professional learning team approach. The programs we have in place are only as good as the people you have running them, and we put those most committed to student achievement into our workshop classes.

And the impact of these changes on Forest Grove's culture?

- Higher academic expectations for all students.

- More students passing the state assessments and better prepared for "stretch" learning opportunities.

- More students enrolled in AP and more AP classes offered.

- Gains in the graduation rate and the college-going rate (with many more students receiving scholarships and awards). In fact, this year a community member donated $1 million to establish a new college scholarship as a direct result of seeing the dramatic improvements made at the high school.

Change Leadership Activities: Explore Possible Solutions

This element of the change leadership process focuses on the generation of multiple approaches for addressing the issues and goals you identified based on your data analysis. It ensures that no stone is unturned in selecting the best approach for your issues, goals, and school culture. It is important at this time to keep an open mind about what might work in your environment. People don't know what they don't know, but they can become informed of options so the best ones can be selected. When your team has landed on the approach that best meets your needs, you must create a compelling vision of your goals and why the approach selected is the one that will bring results. Some of the keys to success include:

- Investigating a wide range of options that include involving people in activities they enjoy, e.g., school site visits, research on best practices, interviews, focus groups, speaking with experts, attending workshops and showcases, etc.
- Involving others—those not on the *BR* team—in the investigation process, (e.g., inviting them to join a subteam) that will also support the buy-in process.
- Developing sophisticated communication processes.
- Creating and employing a clear set of criteria to evaluate each option's fit for your school.
- Creating a compelling vision for the future of your school once the final approaches have been selected.

As you investigate possible solutions to your challenge, be certain to consider leverage points, described on the Thwink.org Web site as follows:

A **low leverage point** is a place where an amount of force causes a small change to system behavior. A **high leverage point** is a place in a system where a small amount of change force (the effort required to prepare and make a change) causes a large amount of predictable, favorable response. An example of a low leverage point would be pushing on the side of a ship to change its course. It would require a large amount of force to have the intended effect. But if the high leverage point of pushing on the rudder is used instead, it takes only a small amount of force to achieve the same effect.

At a high leverage point a small structural change to a system can cause the system to behave much more favorably. Only the use of the correct high leverage points can solve a difficult, complex social-system problem, because if a low leverage point is used, system resistance cannot be overcome.

Beware! When problem solvers are first exposed to the concept of high leverage points, a nearly universal phenomenon transpires: They start thinking… Where are the high leverage points? Is this one? No, probably not. Well, what about this one? Or this one?

At that point what you are really doing is the same thing you were doing before: creating solution strategies intuitively. You are trying to brainstorm high leverage points, which is the same as brainstorming solutions. If this happens to you, then it will help to realize that high leverage points are not identified by intuitive hard thinking. They are found by calm, prolonged true analysis—

breaking down a problem into smaller problems. If you have not built a good model, or have skipped the analysis step, then the high leverage points will remain as elusive as ever. A good analysis uses a formal, well refined process to drive the analysis—and to find the root cause of the problem. Root causes are found by asking this question repeatedly until you get to the root: "Why is this happening? You are able to stop asking the questions when the root cause you have identified has three characteristics:

1. It is clearly a major cause of the symptoms.
2. It has no productive deeper cause. (The word "productive" allows you to stop asking why at some appropriate point in root cause analysis—otherwise you may find yourself digging to China.)
3. It can be resolved. Sometimes it's useful to include unchangeable root causes in your model for greater understanding. These have only the first two characteristics.

The important thing is to not stop at intermediate causes. These are plausible and easily found. Working on resolving them looks productive and feels productive. Intermediate cause solutions may even work for awhile. But until the true root cause is resolved, the system will invariably find a way to circumvent or thwart these solutions, because intermediate causes are symptoms of deeper causes. One must strike at the root. This is important, because it appears that most efforts to solve the sustainability problem have focused on addressing the symptoms instead of the root causes. (Reprinted with permission)

For example, if your diagnostic assessment (data gathering) reveals that a significant number of students are below grade level—so far below that their problems cannot be addressed by embedding literacy through the curriculum (primary intervention), nor would alternative strategies or tutoring (secondary intervention) help these students catch up, then you might need to explore a separate class (tertiary intervention) for these students above and beyond the core classes. To find out the most appropriate solution, you might conduct informal reading interventions for students who scored one standard deviation below grade level.

For one school principal that meant providing more than 300 students with one-on-one 30-minute assessments. (The district temporarily deployed all reading teachers to the school to help complete the assessments.) But after the assessment was complete and the team understood the challenges involved—students had poor phonic skills, low phonemic awareness, and poor word recognition—they were better able to focus intervention strategies.

Activities: Gather and Analyze Data to Determine Priorities

The following matrix reflects those core change leadership elements and questions that surface during the data gathering stage of the change process. Each section of the process circle has a similar matrix. *(The list below is a sample and is not intended to provide all of the information for any given initiative. Tailor it to your school's needs.)* The *BR* team should discuss and complete the activities matrix in each chapter. This exercise will help to ensure that your team has considered most areas related to the initiative. A sample of what a combined activity chart might look like can be found in the last section "Tying It All Together."

<table>
<tr><td rowspan="5">Essential Elements of Each Step</td><td>Sources of Data and Analysis</td><td>
■ Have you reviewed all the BRII and BRIM strategies and recommendations?
■ Have all the possible solution approaches/options been identified for data collection, e.g., curriculum, instruction, assessment, scheduling, professional development, equitable access to programs, academic support, and specific programs such as advisories or student-led conferences?
■ Have data collection protocols been created when investigating different options. For example, is there a protocol for school site visits or for the analysis of presentations at school showcases?
■ Have clear criteria been created for evaluating options with regard to their potential for meeting your school's needs?
■ Have team members been trained in how to use the criteria to evaluate the options?
</td></tr>
<tr><td>Collaborative Leadership</td><td>
■ Are you able to offer different stakeholders leadership roles in the investigation of options? For example, have you assigned a leader for the school site visit team, or assigned a leader of a research team who will be scouring the literature for options that have been successful in schools like yours?
■ Have people been assigned to take a lead in communicating findings to stakeholders?
■ What role are students playing at this stage in the process?
■ Have you considered putting students in charge of any of the site visit teams?
■ Have you considered having students do site visit report presentations?
■ Have you invited students from other schools to do presentations to your staff on successful programs in their schools?
</td></tr>
<tr><td>Infrastructure Capacity</td><td>
■ As you look at options, are you considering how they will impact job roles, policies, procedures, and other practices?
■ Do any of the options being considered require a change in your communication or decision-making structure?
</td></tr>
<tr><td>Communication and Buy-in</td><td>
■ Are you keeping up with your communication requirements?
■ Are you sitting down with key stakeholders, particularly those who are resistant, to keep them on board with your efforts?
■ Based on the options selected, have you created a truly compelling vision of how those options will meet your goals?
</td></tr>
<tr><td>Professional Development</td><td>
■ Have people been given the skills necessary to collect data on different approaches/options.
■ Have they been trained on how to use data collection protocols?
</td></tr>
</table>

Activities: Gather and Analyze Data to Determine Priorities

Worksheet

(Note: An electronic version of this worksheet is available at www.principals.org/brguide)

Sources of Data and Analysis	
Collaborative Leadership	
Infrastructure Capacity	
Communication and Buy-in	
Professional Development	

Essential Elements of Each Step

Challenges and Tips: Explore Possible Solutions

1. *BR* team should designate a person to lead the investigation of possible solutions because it requires significant planning, organization, and coordination.

2. At this point in the process, it's easy to feel overwhelmed. The investigation of options takes considerable time and effort, so be sure to invite stakeholders who are outside the project team, including students, to assist in the process.

3. Investigating and generating options offers wonderful opportunities to engage potential resistors in the process. It is very common for those who are resistant to be completely turned around when they see what is possible. For example, it is not uncommon for many teachers to be resistant to advisories. But if they get the chance to visit schools with successful advisories and speak in-depth with students and teachers, they almost always become supporters.

4. Be prepared when conducting site visits. Be sure to use protocols for your data collection efforts to ensure that time is focused on what's most important. Everyone's time is precious—even more so in schools that are visited often. In many cases, schools with benchmark programs will charge you to visit their schools to help defray the cost of spending time with you.

5. Bring students on your site visits.

6. While on a site visit, it is typical for a school to tell you only about their success in what they are doing. Be sure to ask about the challenges and failures they encountered in the process of developing a successful program. Also ask them how long it took. Most people assume that program implementation can happen more quickly than what is realistic.

7. Although it is more typical to visit schools, consider having individuals from the schools visit you to present their programs. That gives you the opportunity to have a broader audience hear the success story and feel part of the process.

8. Once you have all your data, take time to analyze it well, because you need to build a strong case for the approaches your team recommends for your school. If you can't support the approaches with credible data, you won't be able to craft a compelling vision and generate the necessary buy-in. At this point, you have to be able to prove that the payoffs—for all involved—far outweigh the perceived costs of making the proposed changes. A thorough analysis at this time also enables you to accurately gauge your level of readiness for implementation—a topic that is addressed in Chapter 6.

9. Build a compelling vision that explains your recommendations and present this vision to your key stakeholders. Your vision must clearly describe why you believe the approaches are the most appropriate and can be accomplished at your school. How this is done should be reflected in your communication and buy-in plan and should involve one-on-one and focus group meetings with your most important stakeholders.

10. Perhaps most important, continue to educate your stakeholders about the change leadership process, where you are in that process, and where you are going next (i.e., readiness and capacity building). Invite those who might be inclined to help in that process.

11. Conduct student forums to explore student ideas. (Visit www.nasc.us/rsvp.)

When Things Go Wrong

The following example provides evidence of what happens when the team development, communication and buy-in, and data collection and analysis processes have not been adequately addressed at this point in the change process.

Fighting City Hall

A number of years ago, in an urban area that was losing population, there were three magnet schools (liberal arts, science, and technical) with a total population of 1,100 students. For financial, not pedagogical or social reasons, it was decided to expand the plant of the largest school and bring the three schools under one roof with a single administrative structure and three houses that maintained the same theme as before. No one was really happy with the results. Problems grew under this structure and included unequal access, racial tensions—all the minority students were in the technical house and large achievement gaps existed between the technical house students and those of the other two houses—lack of teamwork among staff members and leadership that never could seem to improve the climate or performance. There was a lot of talk about change but little action.

The district, with support from the community, decided to bring in a progressive educator and leader to initiate a broad school redesign improvement process at the beginning of the following school year. The top candidate accepted the position only on the condition that he be allowed to do the following:

- Eliminate the current themed houses and institute three smaller learning communities to which students would be assigned randomly. These would be schools with their own deans, administrators, and teachers.

- Establish a four-year advisory program.

- Institute collaborative planning time—while fostering a professional learning community.

- Introduce and enhance teachers' ability to present differentiated instruction supported by professional development.

- Hire all the staff as positions became open.

The conditions were agreed to and he accepted the position. Soon after taking the job, he pulled together a broad committee of people willing to work on the redesign, asked for and received technical assistance, and jumped right into the design process. This included conducting sessions to educate teachers and parents about the proposed changes. Although he was aware that not all the teachers and parents were on board, he decided that the new design would be implemented by the start of the next school year.

In the spring before implementation, he hired three highly qualified deans, one for each of the school communities. At the same time, a method was chosen for distributing students to make each school's population reflect the overall population of the school. Over the summer, all the teachers' rooms were changed.

When students arrived at the start of the next year, they were a very unhappy bunch— expectations for performance had been raised and they were not with their typical cliques—their comfort zone had been disrupted in many ways. The teachers also weren't happy with the change in relationships and loss of their comfortable niches. The pressure of having to deal with heterogeneously grouped classes was very difficult for a majority of them. In addition, many were uncomfortable in their advisory role. Finally, some parents started to complain that their children were going to be disadvantaged by being mixed with the other students. The principal's response to criticism of why all the changes had to be done so quickly was that the lack of equity just couldn't be tolerated a minute longer, regardless of the initial problems the changes might cause.

Although progress was made with some students, some teachers, and some parents, the resistance to the changes was significant, and the effort to keep the enthusiasm and momentum for change rolling was enormous. Within three months of initiating the changes, the school committee, at the urging of influential parents, indicated they were considering a ruling to reintroduce a choice of schools for the next ninth-grade cohort. The principal tried in vain to urge the committee not to do that, and organized some teachers and parents to push back. But the choice ruling was made. Shortly thereafter, the superintendent intervened in some hiring decisions, and made it clear that the principal's hiring authority would be limited.

The principal submitted his resignation because of the lack of support for his vision and authority. When asked, he said he didn't have the energy to continue "fighting city hall." He finished out the second year, and left even though there were a number of students, teachers, and parents who tried to convince him to stay. Since his departure, some of the changes have been continued, and small performance gains have been realized, but the gains are far below expectations.

A Critique

Why did all the best intentions coupled with practices that had been successful in other environments not have the desired effect? Let's take a look in the context of the success factors. (See p. 92 for Success Factor Checklist.):

- The impact of change was underestimated and not planned for. The principal underestimated the effort it would take to maintain support and momentum for change. The principal failed to recognize the power of collaboration.

- There was no plan for quick wins that would support the value of the changes for teachers, students, and most of all, parents.

- The case for change was not strong enough. The cost of change was perceived by influential parents as too high compared to the payoff. And the payoff was not going to be immediate.

- The principal didn't stay the course; he was not prepared to compromise to make gains on a longer time horizon. He left even though there was support—the personal price became too high.

- It was a critical mistake to take on so much change all at one time and so fast. Not taking on so much in the beginning to allow time to get small wins; make the hill not so steep; and most important, to build support among parents was key to success in this environment. Even though all the practices and intentions were the best, the influence planning and timing was not as effective as it needed to be. He failed to follow the Process Circle.

- It is not clear that the principal created a support team that would take some of the pressure off him. It appears he took on too much himself. Again, a lack of collaboration.

- There was no formal communication and buy-in plan and no communication team.

- There was no effort to conduct role/position design analyses for people affected by the change. Had stakeholders been involved in this process, there would have been more buy-in and increased role demands would have become obvious early on—and could have been dealt with appropriately.

- An effective influencer would have recognized that the changes being implemented would not have obvious immediate gains, and given the resistance to be encountered, built in some type of small wins early on to build support for longer term gains.

- Technical assistance around the change leadership process was not sought.

- The principal demonstrated some sophisticated influence skills, but did not take the longer view of someone who is a strong influencer by nature, which includes knowing and accepting when to give up specific battles to eventually win the war. He did not appear to be someone who lived and thrived on influence challenges which, given how this situation was structured, was essential.

- The principal did not have models to understand and predict individual, team, and organizational behavior and resistance, particularly the degree of resistance. Having a worthy vision and goals are not sufficient.

Bottom Line: This was an unfortunate, but predictable outcome given the situation.

Change Leadership Tools: Explore Possible Solutions

On the following pages are tools and other materials that will assist you during this phase of the change process:

Chapter 5:
Explore Possible Solutions

- Solution Options Generation
- Site Visit Report Elements

Note: Due to various circumstances at individual schools, the tools are not necessarily provided in the order in which a team would use or administer them. In addition, it is likely that not every tool is appropriate for every school. Additional tools that can be conveniently completed online are available at www.principals.org.

Solution Options Generation

This matrix ensures that you are aware of all the options available to you and provides the basis for a plan for generating approaches. For example, a *BR* team at a middle school may choose to conduct focus groups of recent graduates or their parents to discover perceived weaknesses in a given area. It is important that you look at all stakeholders and determine the best way to approach each.

Data Sources/Types \ Strategy	One-on-one meetings	Focus groups	Exercises & exhibitions	Site visits	Workshops, showcases, or summits	Surveys	Research best practices books/arts/ videos
■ Current students							
■ Recent grads in school							
■ Recent grads in workforce							
■ Parents							
■ Teachers							
■ Administrators							
■ Other school staff							
■ District administrators							
■ Other district staff							
■ School committee							
■ Union							
■ Higher education							
■ Accrediting body							
■ Community—business							
■ Community—political							
■ Community—media							
■ Other							

Site Visit Report Elements

This document provides a framework for your site visit. Create a protocol to fit your needs. When you have identified the type of information you are seeking, send it to the schools you are visiting. They will appreciate it and be more prepared to give you what you need while you are there. The more effort you put into planning the visit in your search for possible solutions, the more productive your visit will be in reaching your team's goals. (A more detailed version of this site visit report can be found at www.principals.org)

NOTE: YOUR OBSERVATIONS AND CONCLUSIONS MUST BE SUPPORTED WITH DATA

1. School Visited:
   - School demographics

2. Program Description:
   - Program owner
   - How long in place
   - Key elements
   - Students impacted (all, by grade, etc.)
   - Staff impacted/involved
   - How success is measured and program success to date (in the student outcomes categories—and other measures employed by the school)
   - What accounts for program success, e.g., specific resources, program design, collaboration, student focus, feedback mechanisms, professional development, community involvement, etc.

3. Program Issues:
   - Implementation hurdles
   - Ongoing problems
   - Costs
   - Compromises and adjustments required

4. Program Impact:
   - Student Impact Chart

5. Fit for Our School:
   - Program elements that have promise and those that don't (and why)
   - Potential implementation hurdles

6 Assess Readiness and Build Capacity

It isn't that they can't see the solution. It's that they can't see the problem.

—*G. K. Chesterton*

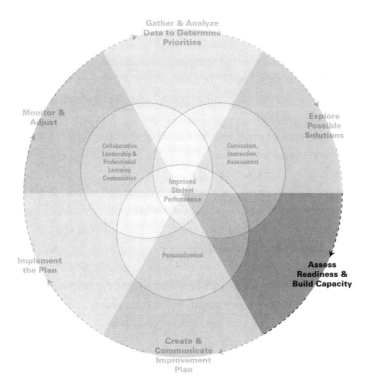

By this point, your *Breaking Ranks* (*BR*) team is well on its way to meeting its change expectations, after it has set goals based on good data and identified an approach and intervention options that will meet the school's needs. If the team has involved key stakeholders in the process and communicated effectively, it has created some buy-in for the goals and approach. But rest assured, not everyone will be on board yet with what your team plans to do. They may feel that the goals and approach make sense, but they may still have concerns about the team's ability to implement it well and to sustain it. In addition, there will be concerns (often unspoken) about what the change will mean for them personally with regard to their roles, relationships, skill requirements, and the amount of work they are going to be asked to do. They will also be looking for evidence that this new approach will work. Finally, even if the team has done everything right so far, this is the point where the initiative or team may have to pay for the sins of the past. To illustrate this point, consider the following quote, which reflects a sentiment one researcher has heard from hundreds of teachers:

When I was told we were introducing a professional learning community program, the first thing that came to mind was, "Oh boy, here we go again—flavor of the month." I'm not saying the program might not be a good idea, but I've been a teacher here for 22 years and have seen at least a dozen programs come through the door—integrated science, project-based learning, writing across the curriculum, technical reading, removing tracks, AP for every student— you get the picture. And you know what—not one of them is around today! With everything I've already got on my plate, I can't get too worked up about anything new at this point. So, when I hear something "new" is coming, my approach is to wait it out, as it will eventually go away—it's not worth getting excited about or putting in the effort.

The question becomes why didn't some of these seemingly good initiatives work and become sustainable at this school? In many cases, it was not because the school was not ready but rather the people were not prepared and the capacity had not been built to a point to sustain the change.

There are several types of readiness that must be evaluated and responded to in preparation for change. The first, as noted above, is related to buy-in. If your school has a negative change history and your staff is not ready to embrace the change, they will resist one way or another—actively or passively. The second has to do with role clarity. The team must ensure that everyone whose role is being affected by the change has a thorough understanding of what they are to do differently, what they are no longer supposed to do, and what knowledge and skills are required to be successful. The third has to do with infrastructure capacity. If goals and how work gets done are changing then work processes, policies, procedures, and practices must be modified accordingly. And if those adjustments are significant, the organizational and communication structure may need to be adjusted as well. Once the team has a good handle on the level of readiness, it can build capacity where necessary.

Anatomy of a Change Effort

An Interview with Bobby Ashley, Principal of Ashe County Middle School, Warrensville, NC, a 2008 MetLife Foundation–NASSP Breakthrough School

The leadership team at Ashe County Middle School took on the task of researching a grading scale of 0–4 instead of the current 7-point grading scale. The team showed initial support for the new scale. Because end-of-grade tests are graded on a scale of one to four, the team felt that it would level the playing field of averages, cut the time it takes teachers to average grades, promote a consistent form of formative assessment, and provide an explanation of state alignment of assessment to parents and other stakeholders. But their ability to assess readiness kept them from pursuing courses of action that were not quite "ready for prime time."

What ultimately was the outcome of efforts to change the grading scale?

After researching and debating all sides of the issue, the team concluded that it was not best for students at ACMS because the local elementary schools are on a traditional 10-point scale and the high school is on a 7-point scale. We did not feel it would be fair or productive to move to this scale without alignment with the larger system.

So the system was not ready for the change the school wanted to propose—an external force. How does ACMS determine whether people within the school are ready for change?

Dynamic leadership is the key—not just leadership from the principal or other administrators, but from teacher leaders. Using the leadership team as a driving force for change is necessary. The empowerment—true empowerment of teachers works very well for us. At ACMS, the principal has only one vote on the leadership team. For ACMS, change comes from collaboration among all of us. We involve the stakeholders who are closest to the situation. This process takes longer, involves a larger audience, and must be made with a great deal of trust.

Do you have any advice for other schools related to readiness and capacity?

Including staff in the process of deciding what the school ought to look like is the key to success. Because discussing changes with the people involved is always the best practice, open and honest dialogue helps prepare ACMS stakeholders for any necessary adaptations.

In some cases, the school is not initially ready for the change. Because our staff has incredibly high standards, slowness to change comes from the fear of not being able to excel in the new. Dialogue, research, activities, and introduction of new concepts must take place to ready a school for change. We collectively bring ideas to the table and leave with a clear vision of where we want to go.

Allowing sufficient time to review the suggested change is necessary for moving forward. Waiting for the appropriate time, sharing conversations among faculty, and providing opportunities for the staff to see the need for change is essential for the process. In most cases, we have been able to choose the right time to make the needed changes. Giving time to each change factor, creates the desire for change to come internally. When people see the need for change, the transition is smooth. Our staff motto operates around the idea that, "If we have always done it that way, it is probably wrong." Seeing how much the world has changed makes us aware that we must make relevant adaptations in order for our students to be prepared for 21st century learning.

Trustworthiness from the top down and bottom up creates a climate among the adults of trust and loyalty to the students. When students see the adults working together toward a common goal, it deepens the belief that we are all here to assist children with their commitment to learning. This type of affirmative modeling only impacts the climate in a positive way. Once the changes are in effect and the faculty and staff members start seeing the beneficial results, a new vigor and atmosphere of excitement spreads throughout the school.

Change Leadership Activities: Assess Readiness and Build Capacity

This element of the change process requires a sophisticated understanding of the scope of the potential impacts of your goals and approach. A major change will touch just about every aspect of your school's operations; therefore, the risk of failure is high if you don't pay attention to the ripple effects of the change you are implementing.

Communication and Buy-In: Leadership Capacity Building

- Involve stakeholders—including students—in readiness assessment activities.
- Encourage teachers to evaluate how important the proposed changes are, and how much of a perceived gap there is between importance and current practice. (Large gaps between perceived importance and current practice will garner the most support for action. Keep in mind that the leadership team's perceptions and those of the staff may differ; address that discrepancy so as not to create resistance.)
- Enhance collaborative leadership wherever possible in support of the changes by redefining roles, conducting orientation sessions about the roles, and providing the professional development necessary to help staff members succeed in those roles.
- Provide frequent communications to the whole school community on the assessment and capacity-building process.

Role Clarity

Involve stakeholders in the role change analysis and redefinition process.

- Educate everyone on which roles will change and which will not and provide a clear picture of new role requirements. For example, if your school is implementing a schoolwide literacy initiative, all teachers should understand that they are teachers of reading—responsible for teaching the language of their course and helping students understand vocabulary and course content.

Infrastructure Capacity Building

- Analyze how your goals will change the way work gets done across the organization.
- Establish current performance baselines in those areas impacted by your goals.
- Conduct an "off the plate" analysis to adjust priorities and to free up time and resources to support goal attainment. (Seldom do organizations take the time to analyze what activities should be stopped to make time for new activities.)
- Adjust processes, policies, procedures, practices, and structures to support and sustain goal attainment.

Capacity building is most effective when all priorities are abundantly clear and resources can be allocated appropriately. In most cases, new initiatives cannot be added without consolidating efforts or eliminating other duties. To gain full commitment to a new initiative, **it is important to identify what is no longer required**—what people can take off the plate. This can only be done when priorities have been established. The team must clarify all of the demands that are planned and in play at any one time. This allows for appropriate prioritization and resource allocation. As you review these, it would be helpful to engage in an initiative mapping exercise that includes:

1. Brainstorming. Brainstorm all the initiatives—mandated and self-generated—that you are dealing with. Place each initiative on a separate sticky note and then place it on one of three flipcharts reflecting a timeframe, i.e., current/short-term, medium-term, and long-term.
2. Prioritizing. Rank the initiatives in each time period according to impact on student performance (academic, civic, social-emotional, postsecondary readiness, etc.).
3. Analyzing resistance. For each initiative, indicate the amount of resistance expected (low, medium, high), and the owner of each initiative (all noted on the flip charts).
4. Identifying implications. Given your analysis, identify the implications for the new initiatives you are planning and write them on a flipchart. Be sure to note where consolidation or elimination of initiatives is appropriate.
5. Presenting. Be prepared to present your results.

Activities: Assess Readiness and Build Capacity

The following matrix reflects those core change leadership elements and questions that surface during the "Assess Readiness and Build Capacity" stage of the change process. Each section of the process circle has a similar matrix. *(The list below is a sample and is not intended to provide all of the information for any given initiative. Tailor it to your school's needs.)* The *BR* team should discuss and complete the activities matrix in each chapter. This exercise will help to ensure that your team has considered most areas related to the initiative. A sample of what a combined activity chart might look like can be found in the last section "Tying It All Together."

Essential Elements of Each Step		
	Sources of Data and Analysis	■ What type of data do you need to assess readiness? ■ What tools and processes will you employ to assess readiness for change? ■ Have you identified all aspects of your school's functioning that will be impacted by the change: process, policy, procedure, practice, structure, resource allocation, staffing, curriculum, etc.? ■ Have you identified what will no longer need to be done once the initiative has been implemented?
	Collaborative Leadership	■ What opportunities exist for shared leadership at this stage of the change process? ■ Are the current leadership capacity development activities sufficient to support the effective implementation of the goals? ■ What leadership development will be required to *meet* the goals? ■ What leadership development will be required to *sustain* the goals? ■ What role can your students play in assessing readiness and building capacity? ■ Do you have students who are willing to play a part in the professional development of teachers?
	Infrastructure Capacity	■ Are the resources adequate to support the change? ■ To what degree will reallocation of existing resources be needed? ■ What process, policy, procedure, practice, and structural changes are necessary to support the goals? ■ If major system/infrastructure changes are required, what sequence is needed to tackle them and how long will the capacity building process take? ■ Are the roles that will change because of the proposed changes clear to everyone? ■ Do you have a methodology for conducting an effective role redesign process?
	Communication and Buy-in	■ Are as many stakeholders as reasonable involved in the readiness-assessment and capacity-building process? ■ Are the communication requirements being met? ■ Are key stakeholders, particularly those who are resistant, involved sufficiently to keep them on board with the efforts? ■ Is the team taking the temperature of the organization regarding the planned changes? ■ Are all the key stakeholders real partners in the change process at this point? If not, what must be done to get to that level of mutual support?
	Professional Development	■ What specific capacity development is required for critical groups, e.g., teachers and administrators? ■ Is it clear what development is needed first, second, third, etc.? ■ Has the team created an overall staff development plan?

Activities: Assess Readiness and Build Capacity

Worksheet

(Note: An electronic version of this worksheet is available at www.principals.org/brguide)

Essential Elements of Each Step	
Sources of Data and Analysis	
Collaborative Leadership	
Infrastructure Capacity	
Communication and Buy-in	
Professional Development	

Challenges and Tips: Assess Readiness and Build Capacity

■ This is the point at which resistance will truly become an issue, if it hasn't already. Remember: real change doesn't happen without real resistance. Be prepared for it—engage stakeholders in as many aspects of the change process as possible. Recognize staff members who are engaging in the desired behaviors.

■ People get touchy during evaluation of readiness. People may take it as a personal affront when asked whether their organization's current level of competence is sufficient to meet new or revised goals. Review all aspects of the organization from teaching to administration to determine if current practices and structures support or hinder goal attainment.

■ Reduce resistance and gain support by remaining student-centered throughout the readiness- and capacity-building process. For example, as part of the readiness assessment, the entire leadership team or *BR* team and resistant stakeholders should shadow students for a day. It puts things in perspective and provides quality data about what needs to change. In almost every instance, this activity will reduce resistance and generate enthusiasm and commitment to the team's goals. A continued focus on diagnostic information to drive the initiative will ensure that the focus stays on the students.

■ Evaluate how important the proposed changes are to teachers, and compare that to current practice. The greatest support for change will exist where the perceived gaps are largest, and the team will want to use that information in creating the sequence and timeline of change activities. For example, there may be a need to wait a year on a proposed change activity that is not seen as urgent because current practice is perceived as adequate. This will give time for more data to be generated and gathered to build a case for change around that specific activity. A survey tool for this purpose is provided on page 96.

■ Education is famous for adding things to the plate, but never taking anything off. Be sure to adjust priorities to support goal attainment. This usually involves stopping or collapsing and combining some current initiatives. An initiative mapping exercise can be very helpful in accomplishing this.

■ A lack of role clarity is a major contributor to initiative failure. Provide time to examine and if necessary redefine roles in detail, and orient people to changes in their roles by providing professional development to build the skills required by the new role requirements. This not only increases capacity but also builds buy-in through involvement and enthusiasm for the changes.

Potential Rationales for Resistance Include:

■ Broken psychological contract
■ Disagreement with the change
■ Change may impact security—job and/or pay
■ Dislike of person leading the change
■ Moves person out of comfort zone
■ Loss of sense of competence (current expertise not valued any more)
■ Loss of power
■ Requires new skills
■ Fear of rejection or unknown—envision negative outcomes
■ Takes energy to change—current routines/habits
■ Asked to do more—no reward
■ Loss of friends/coworkers
■ People filter the information—often incorrectly
■ Rigid personality/lack of flexibility

Change Leadership Tools: Assess Readiness and Build Capacity

On the following pages are tools and other materials that will assist you during this phase of the change process:

- **Change Leadership Success Factor Checklist**
- **Commitment/Motivation Checklist**
- **Importance Versus Practice:** *Breaking Ranks* **Recommendations Survey**
- **Goal Status Questionnaire**
- **Role Change Worksheet**
- **Leadership Capacity Questionnaire**

Note: Due to various circumstances at individual schools the tools provided are not necessarily in the order in which a team would use or administer them. In addition, it is likely that not every tool is appropriate for every school. Additional tools that can be conveniently completed online are available at www.principals.org.

Chapter 6: Assess Readiness and Build Capacity

Change Leadership Success Factor Checklist

This tool is used to measure the effectiveness of your overall management of the change process and should be used on a regular basis to check on progress.

It is estimated that 80–90% of major organizational realignment or change initiatives fail to meet their goals and in some cases result in disruption and lower performance. The checklist below captures those variables that are related to the success or failure of change initiatives. The list is based on a well-established model of high-performing organizations. Your team should use the checklist at a number of points during a project to evaluate how well you are progressing in addressing each of the success factors with regard to strengths and potential vulnerabilities.

Success Factors	Yes	No	Somewhat
1. Project goals/outcomes are well-defined			
2. The goals/outcomes make sense, i.e., are grounded in proven theory and aligned with stakeholder need			
3. The goals are realistic and include the time frame for implementation			
4. A cost-benefit analysis has been conducted to ensure that the outcomes significantly outweigh the cost of the initiative			
5. A comprehensive and well-vetted project plan is in place			
6. The potential impact on all stakeholders has been identified and planned for			
7. Planned changes enhance the school's/district's core competence and add new competence			
8. Metrics and a system for measuring and tracking the impact of the changes are in place			
9. The initiative has top management sponsorship and support (district as well as school level)			
10. The initiative is adequately resourced (money, people, time, etc.)			
11. The people chosen to plan and execute the changes have the requisite expertise (or will in a short time)			
12. An effective change management/communication plan is in place to foster buy-in and minimize disruption			
13. Change champions are in place throughout the school and district			
14. A skilled change management process owner has been assigned to oversee and execute communications			
15. Process change requirements are crystal clear to include infrastructure as well as core processes			

Success Factors	Yes	No	Somewhat
16. Technology enablement has been identified and planned for re: process improvement support			
17. Policy change requirements are crystal clear			
18. Procedural change requirements are crystal clear			
19. Organizational structure change requirements (authority and communication channels) have been defined			
20. Specific job structure/requirement changes have been defined; role change requirements are clear			
21. Job knowledge, skill, and talent requirements for new or changed positions have been identified			
22. A plan is in place for the evaluation of job incumbents against new position requirements			
23. A staffing plan responding to the changes is in place and addresses hires, fires, and training and development needs			
24. A detailed implementation plan is in place to ensure that nothing important slips through the cracks in transition			

Chapter 6: Assess Readiness and Build Capacity

Commitment To Change: Motivation Checklist (Instructions)

Purpose

- Assess the degree to which your stakeholders have bought into and will be motivated to support your goals.

- Provide the *BR* team with a perspective of what type and how much communication and buy-in work is required for project success.

- Provide a tool that can be used on a regular basis by the *BR* team to assess progress in building and sustaining support for change.

Who

- The *Breaking Ranks* team.

- This may be given to stakeholders to gain individual responses, but is not recommended. Without a common understanding of what the terms mean, the instrument may raise more questions than it answers. It is recommended the *BR* team use the tool to create parameters and standards for their process. The *BR* team should then validate their findings by gathering face-to-face data from key stakeholders—guided by the tool, but not using the tool for data-gathering purposes.

When

- The team should meet monthly to evaluate progress.

How Long

- Ten minutes to administer and 30 minutes to discuss and clarify findings. Creating actions to address the "No" responses will take longer.

How

- Distribute the tool and explain the process: "Read each item and determine the degree to which you feel each statement is a true reflection of how stakeholders perceive the item by circling "Yes" or "No." If you are unsure of an answer, don't understand it, or feel that stakeholders would be mixed on the item, then circle "No."

- When there is doubt, team members are directed to answer "No," as it indicates a potential vulnerability that must be checked.

- If you want to target specific stakeholder groups, then fill out the form for each specific stakeholder group. In the beginning, it usually suffices to consider all stakeholders as a single group.

Processing the Results

- Compare (post if desired) findings and discuss the implication of the "Nos" to project success.

- It is expected that the "Nos" will outnumber the "Yeses" at the beginning of the process and that will change over time as the key issues are addressed to turn each "No" into a "Yes."

- Come to agreement on prioritization and actions required to address the "Nos."

- Take time to put an appropriate time horizon and level of effort on what it will take to get all "Yeses." This will help with your overall planning process.

Commitment to Change: Motivation Checklist

Yes	No	
		1. People understand the need for change.
		2. People have a clear picture or vision of what they must do differently to meet new goals.
		3. People have had input in defining the new goals based upon change requirements.
		4. People have had input into determining how the new goals will be met (the process).
		5. People can identify a personal pay-off for meeting new goals and recognize the consequences of not meeting the goals.
		6. Strategic and tactical/operational plans are in place at all levels to act as road maps to meeting new goals.
		7. People have been given goals that are neither too large (frustrating) nor too small (not challenging).
		8. Models of success demonstrating the new behaviors and practices required to meet goals are clear and present in the organization.
		9. People have been given permission to cease nonproductive behaviors and practices and to drop old paradigms.
		10. People have been shown how to reprioritize their activities based upon the demands for new activities required to meet new goals.
		11. People have been empowered to act on their own to meet goals and to provide input at all levels.
		12. Resources (time, money, coaching, training) have been allocated to support new plan/goal attainment.

Importance Versus Practice: *Breaking Ranks* Recommendations Survey (Instructions)

This tool can be given to any key stakeholder and is used to assess readiness and to generate buy-in. Customize the tool to fit specific needs. Note that there is a space for each survey item and two five-point scales—one for importance and one for demonstrated practice. Each person reads the item, evaluates how important it is for student success, and estimates the degree to which the practice is currently in place in the school.

To customize the survey, identify the key activities and practices involved in the changes the team is proposing, and enter each one as a survey item in the form. This means the team must analyze in detail all the changes that will be required across the school to identify what should go in the survey. Just creating the survey is a valuable activity in and of itself because it helps set priorities and reminds everyone of the scope of what is proposed.

Have different stakeholder groups take the survey and debrief it with them—with a particular focus on large gaps between importance and degree of practice. Identify the implications for readiness to implement the changes. Also pay particular attention to differences across the groups. Every item in the survey has importance in supporting the change goals, so it is crucial to see the degree to which the items are seen as important by the stakeholders. It is also valuable to compare the degree of importance to the degree that stakeholders feel the activity or practice described is already being demonstrated. The bigger the gap, the more buy-in is likely for taking action on the activity or practice described. In addition, the bigger the gap, the more preparation that may be necessary before implementing changes.

Importance Versus Practice: *Breaking Ranks* Recommendations Survey

The scale is 1–5 with 5 being the highest level importance or practice.
Perceived Importance Rating: 5 = Very important   1 = Not important
Actual Practice Rating: 5 = Frequent or common practice at this school   1 = Infrequent or rare occurrence at this school

Collaborative Leadership and Professional Learning Communities	Perceived Importance	Actual Practice	Difference
1. The principal will provide leadership in the school community by building and maintaining a **vision**, direction, and focus for student learning.			
2. Each school will establish a **site council** and accord other meaningful roles in decision making to students, parents, and members of the staff to promote student learning and an atmosphere of participation, responsibility, and ownership.			
3. A school will regard itself as a **community** in which members of the staff collaborate to develop and implement the school's learning goals.			
4. Teachers and teacher teams will provide the leadership essential to the success of reform and will collaborate with others in the educational community to **redefine the role of the teacher** and to identify sources of support for that redefined role.			
5. Every school will be a learning community for the entire community in which professional development for teachers and the principal is guided by a **personal learning plan** that addresses the individual's learning and professional development needs as they relate to the academic achievement and developmental needs of students.			
6. The school community will promote policies and practices that recognize **diversity** in accordance with the core values of a democratic and civil society and will offer substantive, ongoing professional development to help educators appreciate issues of diversity and expose students to a rich array of viewpoints, perspectives, and experiences.			

Collaborative Leadership and Professional Learning Communities	Perceived Importance	Actual Practice	Difference
7. Schools will build **partnerships with institutions of higher education** to provide teachers and administrators at both levels with ideas and opportunities to enhance the education, performance, and evaluation of educators.			
8. Schools will develop **political and financial relationships** with individuals, organizations, and businesses to support and supplement educational programs and policies.			
9. At least once every five years, each school will **convene a broadly based external panel** to develop and deliver a public description of the school, a requirement that could be met in conjunction with the evaluations of state, regional, and other accrediting groups.			
Personalization and the School Environment			
10. Schools will **create small units** in which anonymity is banished.			
11. Each teacher involved in the instructional program on a full-time basis will be responsible for **contact time with no more than 90 students** so that the teacher can give greater attention to the needs of every student.			
12. Each student will have a **personal plan for progress** that will be reviewed often to ensure that the school takes individual needs into consideration and to allow students, within reasonable parameters, to design their own methods for learning in an effort to meet high standards.			
13. Each student will have a **personal adult advocate** to help him or her personalize the educational experience.			
14. Teachers will convey a sense of caring to their students so that students know that **teachers have a stake in student learning**.			
15. Each school will develop **flexible scheduling and student grouping** patterns to meet the individual needs of students and to ensure academic success.			
16. The school will engage students' **families as partners** in the students' education.			
17. The school community, which cannot be values-neutral, will advocate and model a **set of core values** that are essential in a democratic and civil society.			
18. Schools, in conjunction with agencies in the community, will help coordinate the delivery of **physical and mental health as well as social services.**			
Curriculum, Instruction, and Assessment			
19. Each school will identify a set of **essential learnings**—in literature and language, writing, mathematics, social studies, science, and the arts—in which students must demonstrate achievement to advance to the next level.			

Collaborative Leadership and Professional Learning Communities	Perceived Importance	Actual Practice	Difference
20. Each school will present **alternatives to tracking and ability grouping.**			
21. The school will **reorganize the traditional department structure and foster the use of teacher teams** that have ample common planning time to integrate the school's curriculum to the extent possible and emphasize depth over breadth of coverage.			
22. The content of the curriculum, where practical, should **connect to real-life applications** of knowledge and skills, and will extend beyond the school campus to help students link their education to the future and to the community.			
23. The school will promote **service programs and student activities** as integral to an education, providing opportunities for all students that support and extend academic learning.			
24. The academic program will **extend beyond the high school campus** to take advantage of learning opportunities outside the four walls of the building. **NOTE: This recommendation is specific to high school and appears only in *BR II*.**			
25. Teachers will design high-quality work and **teach in ways that engage students**, cause them to persist, and—when the work is successfully completed—result in student satisfaction and acquisition of knowledge, critical-thinking, problem-solving skills, and other abilities.			
26. Teachers will know and be able to use a variety of strategies and settings that identify and **accommodate individual learning styles and engage students.**			
27. Each teacher will have a broad base of academic knowledge, with **depth in at least one subject area.**			
28. Teachers will be adept at acting as coaches and facilitators to promote more **active involvement of students in their own learning.**			
29. Teachers will **integrate assessment into instruction** so that assessment is accomplished using a variety of methods that do not merely measure students but become part of the learning process.			
30. Recognizing that education is a continuum, educators must understand what is required of students at every stage and **ensure a smooth transition academically and socially** for each student from grade to grade and from level to level.			
31. Schools will develop a strategic plan to **make technology integral to curriculum, instruction, and assessment**, accommodating different learning needs and helping teachers individualize and improve the learning process.			

Breaking Ranks: A Field Guide for Leading Change

Goal Status Questionnaire

This questionnaire is designed to provide feedback on how effectively the goal was established, how well the case for change was built, and how ready the team is to implement the changes. Responses to the questions will help the team update the communication and buy-in plans and ensure that key change process factors have not been missed up to this point.

The following items are related to the goal/change initiative that has been selected or is being contemplated for implementation. Read each statement and indicate your level of agreement as it pertains to your current situation, i.e., circle the appropriate number where 1 = disagree and 5 = agree.

Goal Identification and Agreement	Disagree				Agree
1. The issues and problems are clear, and their relationship to student outcomes has been established.	1	2	3	4	5
2. The issues and problems make a compelling case for change that everyone buys into.	1	2	3	4	5
3. The possibilities for change/solutions are supported by research and were thoroughly investigated prior to incorporation in the final goal/intervention.	1	2	3	4	5
4. There is consensus on the goal/change selected for implementation.	1	2	3	4	5
Goal Benefit and Reality Check					
5. The benefits of the goal/change clearly outweigh the risks and costs associated with the change.	1	2	3	4	5
6. The fit of the selected goal/change with other demands and initiatives is clear and planned for.	1	2	3	4	5
7. An appropriate timeline for implementing the change has been set, i.e., sufficient time has been allocated given everything else that is going on	1	2	3	4	5
8. The capabilities of the people and the organization are sufficient to accomplish the goal—we are legitimately ready to take on this goal/change.	1	2	3	4	5
9. Sufficient resources are available to implement the change/goal.	1	2	3	4	5
10. All things considered, the change/goal we selected is the right one and can be implemented and sustained effectively.	1	2	3	4	5

Role Change Worksheet (Instructions)

Purpose

- One of the main contributors to project failure is the lack of role clarity. This tool ensures that role changes are recognized and addressed appropriately.

- Another contributor to failure is not removing former responsibilities as new duties and responsibilities are added. This tool helps identify what no longer should be done as well as what is new to the role or position.

- The tool can also be used to describe the parameters of a new role or position.

Who

- As a dry run, the *BR* team should fill out a form on every position they feel will be significantly impacted by the proposed changes (provides perspective on breadth of change and ensures that changes that impact the union contract are addressed appropriately).

- Once a general picture of the scope of change has been identified by the *BR* team for all key positions impacted, separate role change workshops should be conducted for each of the roles or positions impacted. Workshops should include representatives from the *BR* team, incumbents of the role being impacted, supervisors of that position, and other stakeholders significantly impacted by the role, e.g., if it is the teacher role, students should also participate in the role analysis workshop.

When

As soon as it is clear which positions will be impacted and the nature of the changes are well understood—but well before implementation.

How Long

- 2–3 hours.

How

- Start with the most critical stakeholder group impacted by the changes.

- Break into three subteams (4–6 people per team) ensuring there is a role/position incumbent and a mix of key stakeholders on each.

- Distribute the form and explain the type of information requested in each cell

- Before starting the exercise, explain the proposed changes in enough detail that people will have sufficient data to fill out the form (purpose, content, organization, assessment, and leadership elements of the program).

- Ask each table to analyze the first five role elements. Then compare results and come to consensus on elements 1–5 (post for all to see).

- Based on the consensus for items 1–5, ask one table to analyze item 6, another table to analyze item 7, and the final table to analyze item 8.

- Review results and come to a consensus on elements 6–8 (post on the wall for all to see).

- As a large group, identify what professional development is required to address role/position changes.

- Repeat the workshop/process with the next most important stakeholder group impacted by the changes. The only difference is that you will provide them with the analysis done by the first group.

- Repeat and refine all role/position analyses.

Processing the Results

- Build action items into your overall implementation plan to address the needs identified during the role/position analysis sessions.

- Be sure to communicate your workshop findings to all interested stakeholders.

- Keep in mind that you may need to make refinements to the roles/positions you analyzed based on subsequent stakeholder role/position analyses.

Role Change Worksheet

Role Element	Now	After Change	Comments
1. Outcomes Reflecting Success (Measurable)			
2. Most Important Contacts/Interfaces			
3. Most Important Tasks/Activities/ Responsibilities			
4. Workload			
5. Special Requirements			
6. What Is No Longer Required—Comes Off the Plate	N/A		
7. Authority—Final Word On			
8. Primary Knowledge, Skill, and Talent Requirements			
9. Professional Development Requirements	N/A		

Leadership Capacity Questionnaire

This questionnaire provides a look at leadership practices that support change, regardless of the nature of the change. When analyzing the questionnaire results and assessing implications for the change goals, look at implications in the context of the different sections of the questionnaire. Be sure to consider what the implications are for getting buy-in and support for goal attainment if you get low scores in any of the sections. If leadership capacity is not at the readiness level your team feels necessary to begin the process, identify and plan development activities required before implementing the changes.

The following items are related to the current state of leadership at all levels within your organization. The statements reflect critical issues related to the effectiveness of leadership and its impact on your culture. Read each statement and indicate your level of agreement as it pertains to your current situation, i.e., circle the appropriate number where 1 = disagree and 5 = agree

Goal Focus	Disagree				Agree
1. Leaders build and maintain a vision, direction, and focus for the organization and student learning—to include everyone's role in that vision	1	2	3	4	5
2. Organization and department goals are clear and aligned	1	2	3	4	5
3. Leaders ensure that important conversations, e.g., student achievement and civic and social growth, are always at the forefront, and taking place on a regular basis	1	2	3	4	5
4. Leaders demonstrate positive and high expectations	1	2	3	4	5
5. Leadership models the values and behaviors that support student and teacher achievement, and collaboration at all levels	1	2	3	4	5
Collaborative Leadership					
6. Decisions are shared whenever practical and people are empowered to make decisions at every level whenever possible	1	2	3	4	5
7. Vehicles are in place to enable shared/collaborative leadership and decision making	1	2	3	4	5
8. Leaders support creativity, innovation, and appropriate risk-taking in the service of meeting students needs	1	2	3	4	5
9. Leaders encourage and support people who are willing to step up and take on leadership roles	1	2	3	4	5
Management					
10. People are treated fairly, e.g., workload equity is addressed in an appropriate manner	1	2	3	4	5
11. Leaders manage conflict effectively	1	2	3	4	5
12. Leadership recognizes and acts upon the need to take things "off-the-plate" when additional responsibilities are assigned; people are given permission to let go of old requirements/practices	1	2	3	4	5

Goal Focus	Disagree				Agree
13. Leaders have an accurate view of what is going on, i.e., individual or group needs and concerns	1	2	3	4	5
14. Leaders stay in touch with people and get out from behind their desks	1	2	3	4	5
15. Leaders don't shy away from the tough decisions—they use their authority appropriately	1	2	3	4	5
16. Leaders don't initiate major projects without getting the requisite buy-in and doing all the homework necessary to ensure success	1	2	3	4	5
17. Leaders maintain objectivity and an appropriate concern for the well-being of others, even under trying conditions	1	2	3	4	5
Development					
18. There is an ongoing and effective process by which it is determined who needs leadership development	1	2	3	4	5
19. Leadership training exists and is effective for all.	1	2	3	4	5
20. Sufficient resources and time are allocated for leadership training and development for all as appropriate.	1	2	3	4	5
Culture (a reflection of leadership)					
21. Students needs are put ahead of adult needs	1	2	3	4	5
22. People trust, respect, and support one another as peers and across levels	1	2	3	4	5
23. People focus on the future and getting better, versus the past and blame	1	2	3	4	5
24. People respect the authority and communication "chain of command"	1	2	3	4	5
25. People feel comfortable to speak freely to express new ideas	1	2	3	4	5
26. People are prepared for and on time to meetings	1	2	3	4	5

7 Create and Communicate Improvement Plan

Success is only another form of failure if we forget what our priorities should be.

—*Harry Lloyd*

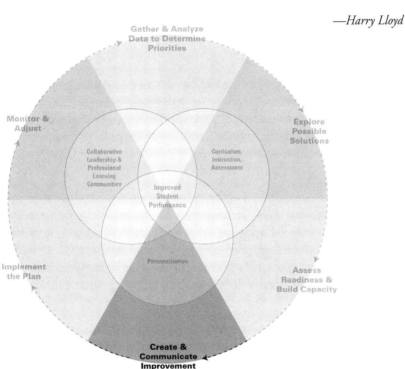

The *Breaking Ranks* (*BR*) team now has all the information it needs to craft and execute an implementation plan. The goals are clear and the readiness assessment has pointed out what capacity building is necessary to get the ball rolling. Once again, the temptation is to race to the finish line. Caution: resources will always be in short supply and buy-in will always be an issue. Managing resources and buy-in requires a good plan and excellent communication. If you are like most of us, you have been exposed to planning that has been less than effective or motivating, as reflected below in the words of an assistant principal:

Planning is a royal pain…and a waste of time. When you're done, it doesn't do anything but confirm what you already knew. I don't think I've ever seen a plan get used. It's put in a drawer until it's time to dust it off and create a new one. People go off and do what they were going to do anyway. Now, you tell me, is that worth spending my time on?

Does this sentiment sound familiar? Even those people who plan well admit that planning is a chore—but an essential one when instituting changes that will have a significant impact. Planning is not a goal unto itself. Plan only to the degree necessary to meet the goals and ensure that what goes into the plan is relevant. Proper planning will help meet and sustain goals through the appropriate allocation of resources and buy-in by those affected by implementation. It may help avoid being blind-sided and provide contingencies for managing the risks associated with change. The following story is an example of how the communication and planning for the improvement were inadequate. As a consequence, the initiative failed.

A Good Idea Gone Bad

The principal of a large inner-ring middle school attended a conference and learned about the positive impact of advisories on school climate, student achievement, and staff commitment in another middle school of similar size and community characteristics. She talked at length with the enthusiastic principal and school staff members who made the presentation at the conference and arranged to visit the school to observe their advisory program in action.

Upon her return to school, the principal presented her advisory revelation at a faculty meeting and stated her intention to build an advisory period into the schedule for the coming year. During the spring and summer, she worked with the administrative team and guidance staff members to build a master schedule into which the advisory period seemed to fit best. In her letter to teachers before the beginning of school, the principal announced that advisories were now a de facto part of the school program. There was a little grumbling and complaining but it was heard as "return to work blues."

During pre-school preparation days, many teachers expressed a variety of concerns about the advisories. The principal responded with answers that she had learned from her observation of the successful program in the other school. During the first week of school as students reported to their advisory assignments, teachers were ill-prepared to begin a positive experience since they did not have an understanding of what they were to do, a commitment to the rationale for advisories, or a structure for accomplishing the principal's intended purposes.

For some of the teachers, the advisories began with positive results in student-teacher relationship building. That, however, was the exception. The principal met with teachers and from their input decided to change the master schedule to have the advisories meet in a different time frame for a shorter period of time. The shorter time period was welcomed by those who were struggling with their advisory group and was frustrating to teachers who had begun working with their advisory students in meaningful ways.

Near the end of the first semester, frustration among the staff was high. Discipline referrals and class cuts during advisory period were at a higher level than any other part of the school day. Parents had begun to complain about students' wasted time during the advisory. After listening to input from teachers, students, and parents, the principal made the decision to revamp the master schedule to eliminate advisories at the end of the semester.

Critique

Who could argue with the concept of children being connected with adults who serve as role models? Who could argue with the idea that adults who work in schools are in an excellent position to provide formal and informal guidance to students outside of the usual relationships that occur between teachers and students? And who could argue that formalizing this process via structures that are supported by time and other resources should not be pursued?

Answer: Those teachers and other adults who work in the school but were left out of the discussion and planning that went into the creation of advisories. This is not the only story of failed advisories, but the issues are often the same. Someone thinks the idea of advisories is a good one and introduces it with little collaborative planning. The teaching staff is expected to implement the plan with little or no preparation. The students are placed into advisory groups in such a way as to make them feel it's something being done *to* them rather than *for* them, and the result is that the very concept of an advisory program, which no educator would argue with in theory, becomes emblematic of "a good idea gone bad."

The change leadership activities in the next section will help your initiatives avoid a similar fate.

Change Leadership Activities: Create and Communicate Improvement Plan

This element of the process provides a safety net. It ensures that the basics have been covered with regard to resources, buy-in, and unforeseen factors that might disrupt goal attainment. The plan creation can be done quickly, but carefully examining and reviewing the plan will take some time and requires good presentation and communication skills. Some of the keys to success are:

1. Designate someone on the *BR* team to be in charge of the implementation planning process.
2. Bring the right people to the table to identify the high level/overarching steps of the plan. This may include additional stakeholders beyond those on the team.
3. Get an individual or subgroup of the team to flesh out the plan.
4. Refine the plan with the whole group that provided the high-level steps.
5. Create a communication strategy for reviewing the plan with key stakeholders.
6. Examine every aspect of the plan with key stakeholders.
7. Refine the plan and communicate it to the whole school community.
8. Establish a vehicle for communicating the plan's progress to the whole community (school and external to the school) on a regular basis.
9. Ensure that the team has designed an effective evaluation process for the plan.
10. Designate a *debugger*—a person well known for finding errors and problems with existing systems. The debugger's role is to find out what's wrong with the plan so that corrections can be made to it before the plan is shared.

Activities: Create and Communicate Improvement Plan

The following matrix reflects those core change leadership elements and questions that surface during the "Create and Communicate Improvement Plan" stage of the change process. Each section of the process circle has a similar matrix. *(The list below is a sample and is not intended to provide all of the information for any given initiative. Tailor it to your school's needs.)* The *BR* team should discuss and complete the activities matrix in each chapter. This exercise will help to ensure that your team has considered most areas related to the initiative. A sample of what a combined activity chart might look like can be found in the last section "Tying It All Together."

Essential Elements of Each Step	**Sources of Data and Analysis**	■ What measures have been identified or created to track program impact? ■ What system has been designed to capture data once implementation has been started to evaluate if the program is meeting goals?
	Collaborative Leadership	■ What opportunities exist to share leadership at this stage of the change process? ■ Have volunteers taken leadership roles concerning key aspects of implementation? ■ What leadership development will be required to meet the goals? ■ What leadership development will be required to sustain the goals? ■ What role can your students play in assessing readiness and building capacity? ■ Do you have students who are willing to play a part in the professional development of teachers?
	Infrastructure Capacity	■ Are the resources adequate to implement and sustain the changes? ■ What support will be required from the district office? ■ What support will be required from external technical assistance providers? ■ Has the team redefined role requirements? ■ Has the team updated processes, policies, procedures and practices? ■ Has the team changed organization and communication structures to facilitate the changes? ■ Does the implementation plan outstrip the team's capacity to manage it? Should you start smaller?
	Communication and Buy-in	■ Are as many stakeholders as reasonable employed in communicating the implementation process? ■ Are key stakeholders, particularly those who are resistant, meeting regularly to remain aligned with the implementation efforts? ■ Was the scope of the implementation plan designed to maximize buy-in? ■ Are there quick wins built in to the plan that can be publicized to generate program support?
	Professional Development	■ What specific capacity development has been initiated for critical groups, e.g., teachers and administrators? ■ What processes are in place to track ongoing skill-development requirements? ■ Has the team initiated an integrated and all encompassing staff development plan?

Activities: Create and Communicate Improvement Plan

Worksheet

(Note: An electronic version of this worksheet is available at www.principals.org/brguide)

Sources of Data and Analysis	
Collaborative Leadership	
Infrastructure Capacity	
Communication and Buy-in	
Professional Development	

Essential Elements of Each Step

Challenges and Tips:
Create and Communicate Improvement Plan

■ Don't engage people in the planning process who have no interest or talent for it. Those who will be most successful enjoy practicing their analytical and diagnostic skills.

■ Don't do the detailed planning with a large group or even the whole *BR* team as this will slow down the process and frustrate most participants. With a group or the *BR* team do only high-level planning (a sample high-level plan is provided on page 112). Assign a small group, or one person, to create the detailed plan that includes contingency plans.

■ Ensure that the high-level planning group has the right stakeholders at the table—which means it may be larger than the *BR* team.

■ Ensure that the implementation plan contains change leadership elements such as communication, buy-in, role clarification, and professional development activities as well as steps focused on program development–related activities.

■ Determine the scope of the change to start with. For example, if you are starting with advisories, is it just with one grade level or all grades at the same time? Two things should be in the team's mind when making this decision:

❑ If you don't have the resources, start small.

❑ Buy-in. On one hand, if resistance is strong, it may be better to start small, ensure successes that can be employed to convince others of the value of the initiative, and thereby enhance buy-in for expanding. However, be careful that your team doesn't create animosity or feelings of being left out if the program is not implemented schoolwide.

■ Review the earlier stakeholder analysis and communication plan and determine the appropriate content and vehicle for communicating the implementation plan to stakeholders. Now that the team is actually going to do something, the potential for resistance skyrockets, as those who have been playing the wait-and-see game must now get engaged. Be sure to provide sufficient time and resources to the buy-in process.

■ As the detailed plan is scrutinized, the team should determine how much of the plan should be shared with key stakeholder groups. There may be a need to modify the amount of content and format for different groups.

■ When the plan is presented to stakeholders, be sure to take thorough notes on reactions. Discuss them immediately with the BR Team and others who have responsibility for communicating and promoting the plan so that adjustments can be made as necessary.

■ Don't rush the process. Successful programs may take 12–24 months to establish the major change and another 24–36 months for the changes to become self-sustaining.

Change Leadership Tools:
Create and Communicate Improvement Plan

On the following pages are tools and other materials that will assist you during this phase of the change process:

- **High Level Implementation Plan Tool (the view from 40,000 feet)**
- **Detailed Implementation Plan**
- **Communication and Buy-In Planning Checklist and Communication Planning Matrix**

Note: Due to various circumstances at individual schools the tools provided are not necessarily provided in the order in which a team would use or administer them. In addition, it is likely that not every tool is appropriate for every school. Additional tools that can be conveniently completed online are available at www.principals.org.

High Level Implementation Plan Tool (Simple)

This plan is completed by the *BR* team or a broader team of stakeholders and provides the basis for a more detailed implementation plan to be completed by a small subteam or an individual. It captures the major steps of the implementation process and identifies the time frame for initiation and completion. It also provides a column for identifying derailers, those situations that could seriously disrupt the implementation process. The derailers need to be spelled out so contingency planning can be built into the overall implementation plan. A sample step is provided.

SMART GOAL/OBJECTIVE (Specific, Measurable, Actionable, Realistic, Time-Phased): _____

Milestones/Steps	Comp. Date	Who Owns & Works On It	Potential Derailers/Obstacles & Influence Requirements	Resource Requirements
1. Tailor implementation plan for presentation to stakeholders.	April 30	*BR* team	Failure to craft the right message and plan for each key stakeholder group will slow down the buy-in process.	Released time for 3 key teachers.
2.				
3.				
4.				
5.				

Detailed Implementation Plan

This planning template contains all the elements necessary to ensure that nothing important falls through the cracks and comes up to bite the project later. This form is completed by a single person or a small team and is guided by the high-level plan created by the project team or a broader stakeholder group. A sample step is provided.

Steps & Dates	Owner & Who Is Working On It	Activities & Deliverables	Challenges, Potential Derailers & Influence/ Communication Rqmnts.	Technical Assistance Rqmnts.
1. Tailor implementation plan for presentation to stakeholders. (April 1–30)	■ Owned by the communication subteam leader ■ Whole subteam working on presentation, materials, and approach	■ Review of the original stakeholder analysis and communication plan ■ Creating specific communication package for each key stakeholder group ■ Determining the best delivery vehicle for each stakeholder group ■ Schedule contacts/presentations	■ There are a lot of people to contact ■ There are still pockets of strong resistance among teachers and parents who feel advisories take away instructional time ■ The union, while having approved advisories, has not been a strong advocate; their communication has been lukewarm at best ■ A lot of one-on-one meetings will be required ■ Need to identify and engage additional informal leaders and potential champions	■ TA provider has a number of examples of communication plans and support materials from other successful advisory programs

Communication and Buy-In Planning

Stakeholders

1. All have been identified and prioritized
2. Needs, concerns, and potential for resistance are well understood
3. Influence and advocacy around the project are well understood
4. Communication and project participation needs are well understood

   - What level of input do they desire?
   - What do they need and want to know?
   - When do they need to know it?
   - How frequently do they want to be engaged/communicated to?
   - What communication vehicles will best meet their needs?

5. A plan is in place for creating buy-in and support
6. A plan is in place to neutralize opposition

Communication Vehicles

1. Face-to-face/one-on-one meetings
2. Group presentation
3. Direct mail
4. E-mail
5. Media
6. Newsletter
7. Web site
8. Bulletin board
9. Communication room
10. Question line (call in)

Communication Management

1. A communication committee is in place with roles well-defined, and a process owner has been assigned
2. The communication process is well defined; policies and procedures are in place

Communication Planning Matrix

- In the first column, put the names/positions of key stakeholders, particularly those resistant to your goals.
- Across the top, list the type of communication vehicles you plan to employ.
- In the cells, indicate which vehicles will be used with which stakeholders.

Solution Options Generation

This matrix ensures that you are aware of all the options available to you and provides the basis for a plan for generating approaches. For example, a *BR* team at a middle school may choose to conduct focus groups of recent graduates or their parents to discover perceived weaknesses in a given area. It is important that you look at all stakeholders and determine the best way to approach each.

Key Stakeholders \ Vehicles	Call	E-mail	Formal Letter	Post on Web site	Formal Report/ Summary Briefing	Face-to-Face Meeting	Focus Group	General Meeting/ Presentation
■ Union Leadership	1. Call Union Head— explain situation and set up meeting		2. Send letter confirming reason for meeting		3. Send summary report with formal letter	4. Meet with leadership to explain goals and approach and to gain support		
■ Department Heads								
■ Parents								
■ Parents								
■ Teachers—All								
■ Guidance Dept.								

8 Implement the Plan, Monitor and Adjust

We realize our dilemma goes deeper than shortage of time; it is basically a problem of priorities. We confess, we have left undone those things that ought to have been done; and we have done those things which we ought not to have done.

–Charles E. Hummel

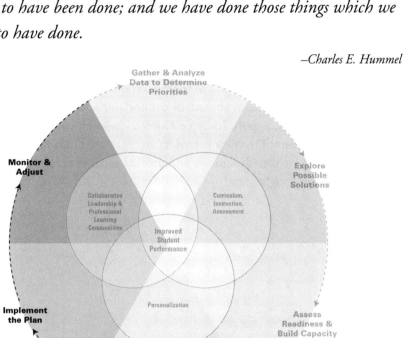

Here we cover the final two stages of the *Breaking Ranks* Process Circle: Implement the Plan; Monitor and Adjust. They are presented together because the minute implementation starts, monitoring and preparing to make adjustments must begin. All of the team's hard work comes down to these stages. Although it's impossible to get everything right or to foresee all obstacles, the work done so far has prepared the team to move forward with conviction and confidence and to weather the inevitable challenges. It is time now for three things: support, support, and more support.

The leader must be ready to take immediate action when things get out of tune (which they will) and people are not reading off the same sheet of music. Once you launch, don't be surprised to hear comments that span the whole negative to positive gamut:

- This is a lot harder than I thought it would be.
- I know we got training on this, but I'm not sure this is really working for me.
- The students keep asking me if this is really necessary.
- I wish we'd had more time to prepare for this.
- I'm going to grieve this!
- Things feel out of synch.
- I'm worn out, but really excited about what's happening!
- The students are nervous about the increased accountability, but they get it.
- The parents are coming around.
- I had a parent tell me her daughter really liked what we are doing.
- We are really focusing on the students for the first time.

Even top performing individuals and teams may be nervous and a bit unsteady on their feet in the beginning, regardless of the professional development or training they have taken. New behaviors aren't smooth or comfortable at first. Think about the last time you took a lesson in a sport. It's typical after a lesson for your performance to get worse for a short time until the new behaviors are integrated into your overall game. You must be ready to make adjustments and provide support to help everyone find their game and bring it to a higher level.

Change Leadership Activities:
Implement, Monitor, and Adjust the Plan

Adjustments are to be expected and will be necessary to ensure sustainability. This is an exciting time, but vigilance is required because regression to old patterns and habits is very easy when things get uncomfortable. Some of the keys to success are:

- Conduct one or two communication blitzes just before implementation to ensure everyone understands what's happening and why.
- Establish a communication process (a weekly newsletter, for example) that keeps everyone informed of the progress on a regular basis.
- Institute effective monitoring strategies the moment you implement.
- Ensure that you are getting real-time feedback on new activities and their impact.
- Identify and publicize quick wins.
- Provide personal coaching and support to those who are most affected by the change.
- Address backsliding the minute you see it.
- Remain vigilant to infrastructure and policy changes that must be made to sustain the initiative.
- Call on expert help.
- Plan for an audit by an outsider to ensure that what the team or school said it was doing is actually being done.

As in previous chapters, the matrix below reflects change leadership elements that are important throughout the change process. The team's ability to answer affirmatively to the questions will ensure that you are on track.

Activities: Implement Plan, Monitor and Adjust

The following matrix reflects those core change leadership elements and questions that surface during the "Implement Plan and Monitor and Adjust" stages of the change process. Each section of the process circle has a similar matrix. *(The list below is a sample and is not intended to provide all of the information for any given initiative. Tailor it to your school's needs.)* The *BR* team should discuss and complete the activities matrix in each chapter. This exercise will help to ensure that your team has considered most areas related to the initiative. A sample of what a combined activity chart might look like can be found in the last section "Tying It All Together."

Essential Elements of Each Step	**Sources of Data and Analysis**	■ Has the team identified all the relevant qualitative and quantitative measures necessary to track the implementation progress? ■ Are there methodologies in place to compile the data and to analyze it quickly so course corrections can be made in a timely fashion? ■ Are data collection and analysis roles clear or in need of adjustment? ■ What are the initial data telling you?
	Collaborative Leadership	■ Is the team sharing leadership as adjustments to the implementation plan are made? ■ Now that you have data, does the team see any new leadership roles emerging as a result of your changes? ■ Students can play a key role in monitoring the implementation process and impact of change. How will you engage them as true partners in the process?
	Infrastructure Capacity	■ Are the resources keeping up with the needs? ■ Have new resource needs been identified? ■ Are there any additional needs for changes in processes, policies, procedures, or practices? ■ Are any additional role refinements necessary? ■ Are any new roles required? ■ Are the changes stretching the staff in any ways that weren't predicted? What will you do if that is the case?
	Communication and Buy-in	■ Are there any quick wins yet, and if so have they been communicated? ■ Is the communication plan being kept current? ■ Is it effective, or does it need adjustment? ■ Are there any surprise reactions from stakeholders? If so, do they require any changes to the communication and buy-in plans?
	Professional Development	■ Are the professional development activities keeping up with the changes? ■ Are the professional development activities being adjusted to meet unforeseen needs? ■ Are experiences with the changes being effectively incorporated into your professional development activities? Are lessons learned being leveraged appropriately?

Activities: Implement Plan, Monitor and Adjust

Worksheet

(Note: An electronic version of this worksheet is available at www.principals.org/brguide)

Essential Elements of Each Step		
Sources of Data and Analysis	
Collaborative Leadership	
Infrastructure Capacity	
Communication and Buy-in	
Professional Development	

Challenges and Tips:
Implement, Monitor, and Adjust

- Ensure that there is a "go-to" person from the project team who is shepherding and monitoring the process and is available and responsive on a 24/7 basis for the first months. (Be sure that everyone knows this is the go-to person.) The leadership team must provide the coaching and moral support at this stage.

- Manage time so that people in key change roles can perform their roles well. For example, have teachers been relieved of nonessential duties, such as study hall and lunch room, to be able to assist in the change process and have adequate time for professional development? If finding the time is difficult, it is worth taking time to do an in-depth off-the-plate analysis to ensure the overall school priorities and allocation of resources will support your change goals.

- Establish a communications center available to anyone interested in the initiative. Make all documentation and resources easily accessible as well as other resources. It is helpful to have the center staffed at all times by a project team member or a member of the communication and buy-in subteam. Resources should be updated and added as necessary.

- Adjust the implementation plan and timeline as necessary. Monitor progress toward milestones.

- "Inspect what you expect." Keep an eye on what's important, and reinforce what's important by being very visible in what is monitored.

- Schedule time to debrief and celebrate the journey at different points in the process (a component of publicizing quick wins). This ensures that everyone stays connected to the process and appreciates that what they are doing makes a difference. Remember that full buy-in takes quite a while.

- Help people take less important activities off their plates. Reinforce the fact that not only do people have permission to drop nonproductive behaviors, but they must do so. Communicate this need and provide examples on a regular basis.

- Make adjustments to keep things on track. This often entails adding activities for which you hadn't originally planned . Be sure to publicize any changes in plans, and provide a clear rationale for the team's actions. If the adjustments involve significant changes, look at this as an opportunity to develop additional collaborative leadership.

- Keep close tabs on resources as you implement, particularly as you make adjustments that require additional resources. If you can't fully provide resource adjustments, you may need to change priorities or the timing of the introduction of new activities.

- Never lose sight of what it takes to sustain a change:
  - Buy-in
  - Bottom-up versus top-down ownership for the changes
  - Goal attainment—it works!
  - The payoff clearly outweighs the cost of implementation
  - Recognition and rewards for those making the changes and showing results
  - Repetition of new practices

- Elimination of old behaviors/practices
- Public commitment to new goals and practices
- Public testimonials as to the positive impact of the change—particularly by prior resistors
- Infrastructure changes that support the changes
- Clear redefinition of roles and refinement based on experience with the changes.

- Look for secondary gains. When progress is made and people buy into the process and outcomes, identify other places in the school that could benefit from the new approach and practices. If you've put into practice all the elements of the change leadership process in implementing a new initiative, you really have instituted a process that supports continuous improvement throughout the school. Be sure to spread the wealth associated with this enhanced leadership and infrastructure capacity.

Change Leadership Tools: Implement, Monitor and Adjust

On the following pages are tools and other materials that will assist you during this phase of the change process:

- **Milestone Tracking Worksheet**
- **Change Activity Impact Worksheet**

Note: These tools are not necessarily provided in the order in which a team would use or administer them. In addition, it is likely that not every tool is appropriate for every school. Additional tools that can be conveniently completed online are available at www.principals.org.

Milestone Tracking Worksheet

Milestones for major change activities were created as part of your implementation plan. This worksheet is a tool to track milestone accomplishment and to note when adjustments are required. Consider posting these worksheets on the wall in the communication center.

Instructions:

- Create a worksheet for each major activity of the initiative, or for each initiative of your overall change process.
- List the milestones developed for that activity or initiative in the left column.
- Fill out the other columns as appropriate with regard to milestone accomplishment.

Major Activity or Initiative:

Milestones	Planned Comp. Date	Met	Not Met	Action Required
1.				
2.				
3.				
4.				
5.				
6.				
7.				
8.				
9.				
10.				

Change Activity Impact Worksheet

This worksheet is a tool for assessing and summarizing the level of proficiency of new activity and practice implementation and the impact on target stakeholders.

Instructions:

- List all major initiatives or major initiative activities and practices in the first column.
- Evaluate the general proficiency with which each initiative or activity is being implemented (high, moderate, low).
- Note the level of impact (+/0/-) on the target stakeholder on four variables: emotion (how do they feel), knowledge (can knowledge acquisition be verified), behavior (are appropriate new behaviors being demonstrated), and outcomes (are the planned measurable outcomes being positively impacted).

Initiatives or Major Activities	Gen. Profic. H M L	Target Stakeholder	Emotion +/0/-	Knowl- edge +/0/-	Beha- vior +/0/-	Outcomes +/0/-	Action Required
1.							
2.							
3.							
4.							
5.							
6.							
7.							
8.							
9.							
10.							

9 Tying It All Together

In Chapter 1, we tackled the importance of changing the culture to support your team's initiatives and overall school improvement. The next chapter introduced the *Breaking Ranks* Process Circle for investigating, launching, and sustaining change. Each of the remaining chapters was devoted to offering your team the information necessary to better plan your initiative given your unique circumstances and challenges. The activities matrix within each chapter encourages your team to ask and answer a variety of questions related to the essential elements of each step—sources of data and analysis, collaborative leadership, infrastructure capacity, communication and buy-in, and professional development.

When you have finished completing each of these detailed sections it should be relatively easy to combine them into one comprehensive activities matrix that gives an excellent overview of the who, what, and how. So what would a version of this matrix look like when you're done? On the next page you will find an example of a literacy initiative aligned with the *Breaking Ranks* Process Circle and the essential elements.

Although a two-page matrix may not detail the depth and breadth of your initiatives nor the work your team has completed in discussing and completing the matrices in earlier chapters, it will give your team and other stakeholders a comprehensive view as well as reassurance that it all fits into a carefully considered and well-developed plan. Following the matrix is a sample plan on advisories that incorporates all of the steps of the process circle in a detailed manner. Remember, if your team has conscientiously tackled the "how" of the initiative, your school is 80% of the way to a sustainable initiative.

The Six Steps: Example—Schoolwide Literacy Initiative

	Gather and Analyze Data to Determine Priorities ➡	Explore Possible Solutions ➡	Assess Readiness and Build Capacity ➡	Create and Communicate Improvement Plan ➡	Implement the Plan ➡	Monitor and Adjust ➡
Sources of Data and Analysis	■ Diagnostic assessment ■ Reading test (SRI, SDRT, Gates) ■ Schoolwide ■ Annual ■ By grade equivalent ■ By lexile ■ Lexile all textbooks	*Breaking Ranks* Culture of literacy Double the work ■ ID preferred diagnostic assessment ■ testing logistics ■ feeder school principal	Diagnostic assessment by grade eq., stanine and lexile	Match student data with lexile levels of textbooks. Make data available to all teachers in electronic gradebook	Plan document including interventions, professional development, assessments, etc. ■ Data indicates widespread issues that exceed the capacity of this or any school to correct at once. ■ Literacy coach to collect data	■ Program audit ■ Diagnostic assessment (annual) ■ Student progress in interventions (monthly)
Collaborative Leadership	Hire literacy coach Form literacy council Principal is part of the LC District approval for diagnostic assessment	Identify tasks and ask literacy council members to volunteer ■ Literacy coach leads meetings	Literacy coach Literacy council Department chairs "Skunkworks" team	Literacy council w/literacy coach as sitting member create plan	■ Literacy coach is the primary backed up by the literacy council. Principals role is to remove barriers and to secure resources	Work with literacy coach takes on appearances of a partnership. Likewise, the literacy coach works collaboratively with the literacy council.
Infrastructure Capacity	Review policies Prepare budget for initial assessments	Literacy coach will need help in navigating various departments and teams with each having different needs and different readiness levels.	Diagnostic assessment data will reveal extent of reading problem	Large numbers of students below grade level. Decisions will need to be made about whom to place in intervention classes.	■ Identify staff members with knowledge in specific areas relative to the identified literacy strategies (vocabulary, graphic organizers, readalouds/thinkalouds ■ One hour per month of required professional development ■ New teachers receive intensified, year-long training ■ Literacy coach is lead mentor	Need exceeds physical capacity. Vertical articulation grows in importance. Meetings held with all feeder school leaders.

Communication & Buy-in	Literacy Council plans staff presentation ■ Newsletters ■ Staff meeting ■ ID driving and restraining forces, teachers on board v. those waiting = new teachers, non-tenured	Set up small meetings to discuss literacy approaches.	Mini-meetings reveal concerns of staff.	Presentation to site council or leadership group	Feedback from site council ■ Modify presentation ■ Strategies identified ■ Training begins ■ Focus long-term ■ Don't force "laggards" or "late majority" ■ Skunkworks team uses experimental strategies ■ Send "innovators" and "early adopters" to outside training	Staff meeting (presentation) ■ Interventions begin at mid-year with no resistance from staff or parents. ■ Monthly training begun ■ New teachers on board
Professional Development	PD survey to construct baseline of teachers' skills (needs assessment) Literacy council conducts training w/council members Survey administrators to determine their readiness levels	Literacy council identifies schoolwide strategies Literacy coach sets up training schedule.	Professional development plan (personal learning plans—PLPs)	A core of strategies is identified for PD of all teachers Content specific needs are identified by the literacy coach and communicated to the literacy council	Innovators and early adopters lead staff meetings under guidance of literacy coach	Professional development is planned a month in advance to keep pace with current issues and developments

Sample Plan for a *Breaking Ranks* Initiative
Advisory Implementation

This school chose to start advisories with incoming freshmen and have students remain with the same adviser for four years. Within four years all grades will have advisories in place. For the sake of brevity, timeframes and potential implementation derailers are not noted. A planning tool addressing these elements is provided on p. 112.

Steps Prior to Implementation Planning

1. The leadership team, through observation and a general review of student data, determines that more must be done to become student-centered and improve the level of personalization.

2. The principal with input from the leadership team creates a *Breaking Ranks* team with key stakeholder representation, to include potential resistors.

3. *BR* team clarifies objectives, identifies and assigns key roles, creates a meeting protocol and schedule, creates an initial project plan, creates a charter, and confirms commitment of all team members.

4. *BR* team conducts a communication/buy-in plan. Additional stakeholders may be added to the team at this time.

5. *BR* team communicates its purpose and goal development process to key stakeholders—and invites participation on subteams as necessary (publicizing the team charter is usually part of this step).

6. *BR* team does a data drill-down to find ways to improve student outcomes and create a more personalized environment.

7. *BR* team collects needs data directly from students and other stakeholders. Stakeholders are invited to participate in the data collection and needs analysis.

8. Based on data, the *BR* team confirms the need for a higher level of personalization, and sets two preliminary goals: teaming of teachers for freshman students and creating advisories.

9. *BR* team communicates the findings of its data analysis to stakeholders.

10. *BR* team conducts best practices research on teacher teaming and advisory programs to identify options. (Stakeholders are involved in this process, to include visits to a half-dozen schools with successful mentoring and advisory programs).

11. *BR* team finalizes its goal and approach—to create an advisory program (but not to do teacher teaming for freshmen at this time)—and communicates this to all stakeholders.

12. *BR* team considers seeking outside technical assistance in its quest to identify and define the five key elements of any effective program: purpose; organization (who, when, time, frequency, etc.); content (academic, social, etc.); assessment (measuring the impact, process for course corrections, etc.); and leadership. Input from successful programs identified in the best practices research and school site visits is built into the program.

13. *BR* team communicates the program design to stakeholders, and makes revisions as necessary.

14. *BR* team conducts readiness assessment and redesigns jobs (with stakeholders) that will be impacted by the change. It identifies how the role of teachers and

guidance counselors will change once advisories are implemented; and includes the identification of any readiness gaps and required professional development.

15. *BR* team communicates the results of the readiness assessment and needs for capacity building to stakeholders.
16. The union contract is modified to account for role changes.
17. Capacity building activities take place.

Implementation Planning

1. Tailor implementation plan for presentation to stakeholders.
2. Update communication plan for the advisory implementation process.
3. Present draft implementation plan (to include the communication plan) to stakeholders—revise as necessary.
4. Revisit the initiative mapping exercise to ensure that priorities for the whole school are clear, make sense, and are used to take unnecessary work off the plate for those affected by the changes.
5. Confirm that there are sufficient resources to carry out the program as designed.
6. Confirm or assign leaders for key elements of the advisory program, e.g. curriculum development, assessment (ongoing monitoring and adjustment), professional development training, and ongoing coaching.
7. Identify and line up internal (district) and external (TA provider) resources as necessary.
8. Continue readiness activities such as infrastructure and leadership capacity building; role redefining; and modifying processes, policies, procedures, practices, and structures to support advisories. Design these changes to ensure program sustainability.
9. Adjust the schedule to accommodate four 25-minute advisory sessions a day immediately after the lunch period.
10. Create or purchase advisory content.
11. Orient teachers to the adviser role.
12. Conduct professional development advisory training (continuation of capacity building) for teachers and for those in program implementation leadership roles (see point 5 above). This includes role clarification and clear permission to discard behaviors and practices that are no longer required.
13. Add information on advisories to the orientation program for eighth graders and their parents, and conduct this orientation program.
14. Conduct advisory kick-off meetings for whole school.
15. Implement advisories.
16. Monitor and conduct debriefs (teacher and students) on a frequent and regular basis for the first three months and less frequently as the program gets its legs under it.
17. Provide additional professional development as needed.
18. Adjust advisory curriculum as required.
19. Communicate progress to whole community and describe successes.
20. Repeat cycle of activities above for next freshman class and new set of teachers moving into the adviser role.

References

ACT. (2008). *The forgotten middle: Ensuring that all students are on target for college and career readiness before high school.* Iowa City, IA: Author.

Balfanz, R., Herzog, L., & Mac Iver, D. J. (2007). Preventing student disengagement and keeping students on the graduation path in urban middle-grades schools: Early identification and effective interventions. *Educational Psychologist, 42*(4), 223–235.

Bennis, W. G. (2008, September). Leadership is the capacity to translate vision into reality. *Journal of Property Management.*

Collins. J. (2001). *Good to great: Why some companies make the leap and others don't.* New York, NY: HarperCollins Publishers.

Fullan, M. (2004). *Leadership & sustainability: System thinkers in action.* Thousand Oaks, CA: Corwin Press.

Fullan, M. (2001). *The new meaning of educational change.* (3rd ed.). New York, NY: Teachers College Press.

Fullan, M. (2008). *The six secrets of change: What the best leaders do to help their organizations survive and thrive.* San Francisco, CA: Jossey-Bass.

Johnson, R. (2004). *Using data to close the achievement gap.* Thousand Oaks, CA: Corwin Press.

Leithwood, K., Louis, K. S., Anderson, S., & Wahlstrom, K. (2004). *How leadership influences student learning.* New York, NY: Wallace Foundation.

Marzano, R. J., Waters, T., & McNulty, B. A. (2005). *School leadership that works: From research to results.* Alexandria, VA: Association for Supervision and Curriculum Development.

McGregor, D. (1985). *The human side of enterprise* (special ed.). New York, NY: McGraw Hill.

National Association of Secondary School Principals. (2004). *Breaking ranks II: Strategies for leading high school reform.* Reston, VA: Author.

National Association of Secondary School Principals. (2006). *Breaking ranks in the middle: Strategies for leading middle level reform.* Reston, VA: Author.

National Association of Secondary School Principals. (2005). *Creating a culture of literacy: A guide for middle and high school principals.* Reston, VA: Author.

National Association of Secondary School Principals. (2007). *Making the mathematics curriculum count: A guide for middle and high school principals*. Reston, VA: Author.

Painter, B., Lucas, S., Wooderson, M., & Valentine, J. (2000). *Turning points recommendation into action: The use of teams in school improvement processes*. Reston, VA: NASSP.

Peters, T., & Waterman, R. H. (2004) *In search of excellence: Lessons from America's best-run companies*. New York, NY: HarperCollins.

Schmoker, M. (2006). *Results now: How we can achieve unprecedented improvements in teaching and learning*. VA: Association for Supervision and Curriculum Development.

Schmoker, M. (1999). *Results: The key to continuous school improvement*. Alexandria, VA: Association for Supervision and Curriculum Development.

Sizer, T. (2002, July). Discover the power of advisories. Presentation at the Serving Smaller Learning Communities Technical Assistance Conference, Providence, RI.

The National Association of Secondary School Principals—the preeminent organization and the national voice for middle level and high school principals, assistant principals and aspiring school leaders—provides its members with the professional resources to serve as visionary leaders. NASSP promotes the intellectual growth, academic achievement, character development, leadership development, and physical well-being of youth through its programs and student leadership services. NASSP owns and operates the National Honor Society®, the National Junior Honor Society®, the National Elementary Honor Society®, and the National Association of Student Councils™.

The Center for Secondary School Redesign Inc. (CSSR) is a leading provider of ground breaking technical assistance to support leadership for personalizing middle level and high schools to meet the needs of every student. CSSR consists of nationally recognized school change coaches who are dedicated, knowledgeable, and passionate about creating personalized and student-centered learning environments. They provide expertise and transferable technology that leads to the development of students' core and 21st century knowledge and skills, social and emotional growth, civic responsibility, and postsecondary preparedness.